THE

AFRICAN

CROSS STITCH

COLLECTION

Dedication

This book is dedicated to all the displaced farmers and people of Zimbabwe.

'That all the good the past hath had

Remains to make our own time glad ...'

The Chapel of the Hermits

First published in 2004 by

Sally Milner Publishing Pty Ltd

PO Box 2104

Bowral NSW 2576

AUSTRALIA

© Trish Burr 2004

Design: Caroline Verity Design

Editing: Anne Savage

Photography: Tim Connolly

Printed in China

National Library of Australia Cataloguing-in-Publication data:

Burr, Trish.

The African cross stitch collection.

ISBN 1 86351 331 0.

1. Cross-stitch - Africa - Patterns. I. Title.
(Series : Milner craft series).

746.443041096

10 9 8 7 6 5 4 3 2 1

THE
AFRICAN
CROSS STITCH
COLLECTION

Trish Burr

SALLYMILNER
PUBLISHING

Contents

7 Introduction

8 Materials and Equipment

11 Hints and Techniques

14 Stitch Instructions

14 Reading a cross stitch chart

14 Getting started

15 How to begin and end cross stitch

16 Basic cross stitch on Aida fabric

17 Cross stitch on evenweave or linen

17 Cross stitch on waste canvas

18 Fractional stitches

19 Backstitch

19 French knot

20 Finishing Instructions

20 Washing and finishing your work

21 Stretching completed work for framing

22 Mounting finished stitching onto card without stretching

23 Making a greeting card

24 Making a bookmark

25 Making a pincushion

25 Making a scissors-keeper or potpourri sachet

26 Making a spectacle case

27 Making a pencil case

28 General Instructions for Working a Design

30 Projects

30 Starter project

32 Sunlight card

34 Twilight card

36 Welcome card

40 Congratulations sampler

44 Welcome sampler

48 Young rhino bookmark

50 Young ostrich bookmark

52 Young warthog bookmark

54 Chameleon bookmark

56 Fish eagle bookmark

58 Big five bookmark

60 Woman with basket bookmark

62 Kudu and cheetah bookmark

64 Guineafowl bookmark

66 Giraffe and rhinoceros bookmark

68 Hippo and waterfall bookmark

70 Ostrich family outing

74 Rhino family outing

78 Warthog family outing

82 Lion family outing

86 Lion's den

90 Guineafowl on parade

94 Giraffe at waterhole

98 Sunshine sampler

104 Motifs

110 Alphabet Chart

111 Acknowledgements

112 Suppliers Index

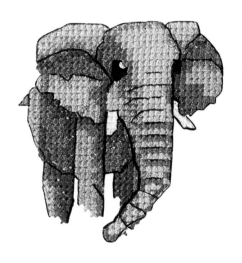

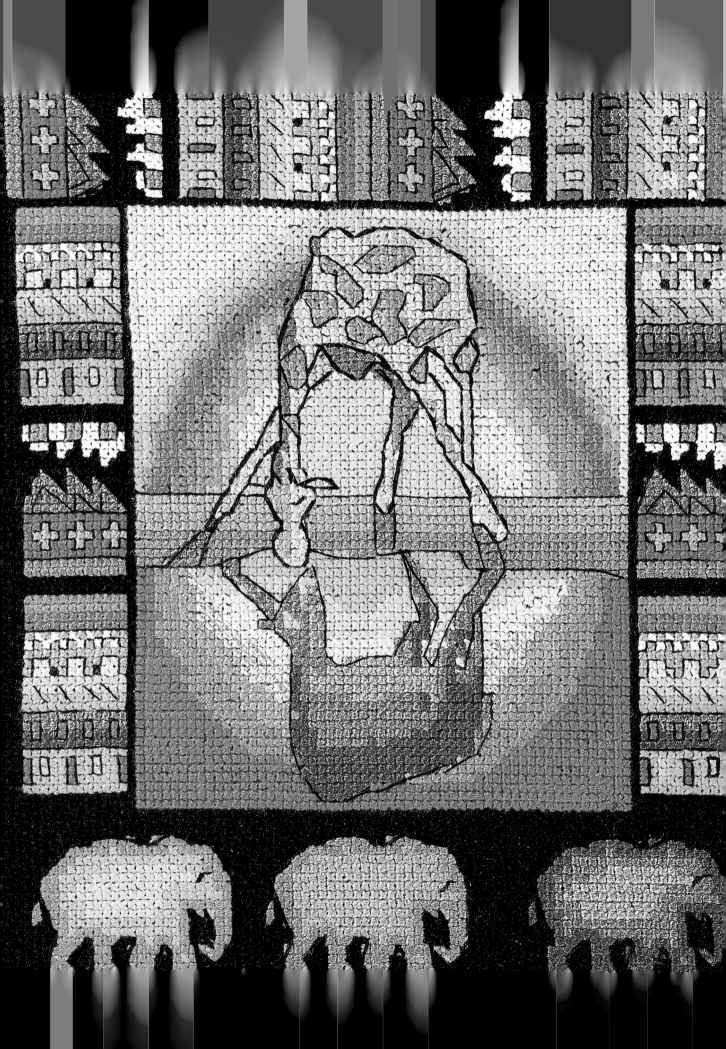

Introduction

The African Cross Stitch Collection is the culmination of years of work and research on African life and its fascinating customs.

I have lived all my life in Zimbabwe, where I was fortunate enough to be brought up on a farm, and later moved to the town of Harare, where I was married and have lived for the past 21 years with my husband and three girls.

Political turbulence has rocked the stability and wonderful way of life in our country, but throughout that time one thing has remained unchanged, the abundance of scenic plant, bird and wildlife that is so wonderful a part of our sunshine-filled environment.

To pay tribute to this background I designed a collection of cross stitch projects intended to depict the enchanting images of everyday life in the southern region of Africa in a semi-realistic, bright, colourful and vivid way, from sunrise to sunset. I have added little folklore stories to accompany some of the designs. I have concentrated on themes from the south of this diverse continent because it is more familiar to me.

I begin with a simple starter project to help you on your way if you have never attempted cross stitch before. The projects progress from quick and easy designs towards more challenging projects for the experienced stitcher. An alphabet chart and library of motifs are included so that you can design your own projects.

I hope that you enjoy these designs as much as I have enjoying creating them.

Materials & Equipment

Fabric

Aida is the most commonly used fabric and is the easiest for beginners. It is made up of woven blocks and cross stitches are made over each block. Aida is available in different counts (HPI, or holes per inch); for example, 14 count, which means there are 14 holes per inch. The common counts are 11, 14, 16 and 18, with 11 count being the largest and 18 count the finest. Aida is available in different widths and colours.

Evenweave is a term applied to a range of fabrics that are woven in single threads rather than in blocks. The cross stitch is made over two threads and covers a nine-hole square. Like Aida, evenweave is available in different counts and colours. The common counts are 28 count (the equivalent to 14 count Aida, as it is stitched over two threads instead of a single block) and 32 count (equivalent to 16 count). It is also available in 25 and 27 count.

Linen is similar to evenweave fabric, although the threads are not evenly woven, and again come in different counts and colours.

The unevenness of the weave gives a slightly irregular finish to the stitching (some people like the natural, rustic character of this finish). Linen is very hard wearing so is ideal for projects requiring durability such as table cloths, but can also look wonderful when used for samplers or framed work. The cross stitches are made as for evenweave.

Waste canvas is used to stitch a design on any fabric that does not have a weave such as cotton, satin, polar fleece, towelling and so on. A piece of waste canvas is tacked onto the appropriate area of the main fabric and the cross stitches are made through both layers. When the design is complete the waste is removed leaving the design on the main fabric. Waste canvas is generally white with a blue or green stripe through it and comes in different counts.

Threads

Stranded cotton is the main type of thread used for cross stitch and is made up of six easily separated strands. The number of strands required for each design can be removed one by one and used together in a needle. Normally two strands of thread are used in 14 count fabric, but I have used three strands in most of the designs to give them added depth.

Stranded cotton is made from long staple Egyptian cotton and is mercerised to give it a sheen. The recommended stranded cotton manufacturers are DMC, Anchor and Madeira as their threads are dyed with highly resistant dyes which ensure colourfastness so that they do not fade with continuous washing and exposure to light. These threads are available in 8 metre skeins and come in a range of around 500 colours. While DMC stranded cotton has been used in all the designs as photographed for the book, I have given the equivalent colour codes for both Anchor and Madeira as well.

Cotton perle has a slight twist and a very pearly sheen. It comes in a variety of thicknesses and is used singly.

Other threads There are a number of other threads available on the market, some hand dyed and some variegated. Make sure that they are colourfast before using.

Metallic threads are available in different thicknesses and colours and can be used alone or combined with stranded cotton to provide a sparkly effect. The recommended brands are Kreinik, DMC, Madeira and Anchor. Kreinik blending filament, which is a very fine metallic thread available in many different colours, is used in this book together with DMC stranded cotton, and DMC metallic stranded is used alone.

Needles

Cross stitch needles or tapestry needles with a blunt point are used for cross stitch. These are available in a number of sizes depending upon the fabric count used. The blunt tip is necessary to prevent piercing the fibres of the fabric and splitting it as you take the needle through the holes. The most commonly used cross stitch/tapestry needles are sizes 24 and 26, although they are also available in sizes 20, 22, 24, 26 and 28. (See the Thread Usage Chart on page 10 for further details.)

Hoops and frames

These are not essential for cross stitching but can be useful to keep the fabric taut while you stitch. Plastic flexi-hoops and wooden hoops with a screw are available in different sizes, alternatively a square or rectangular frame can be used. There are a number of different frames available on the market and the decision is a personal one. If using a hoop it is wise to use one that is large enough to hold the complete design, but if you must use a smaller one and have to move it around while you stitch it is important that you make sure the hoop is clean and remove the hoop when not stitching so that it does not leave marks or distortions on your work. If you do get marks don't panic as they will wash out.

Materials & Equipment

Scissors

A small sharp pair of scissors of the kind recommended for embroidery is essential, and should only be used for cutting your threads. Dressmaking scissors or sharp craft scissors can be used for cutting your fabric.

Masking tape

Masking tape can be used to secure the edges of your fabric while stitching or you can cut the edges with pinking shears to prevent fraying. Products such as Fraystop are also available for this purpose.

Other useful products

There are numerous other cross stitch products available on the market today, including stitching accessories, scissors, finishing accessories, magnifying aids, lighting aids and chart aids. The best ways to find a good selection are to browse the Internet or study the small ads in any good stitching magazine.

THREAD USAGE CHART

Thread	Fabric	Needle	No. of strands
Stranded cotton	Aida 11 count	Tapestry size 22	4
Stranded cotton	Aida 14 count	Tapestry size 24	3
Stranded cotton	Aida 16 count	Tapestry size 26	2–3
Stranded cotton	Aida 18 count	Tapestry size 28	2
Stranded cotton	Evenweave 25 count	Tapestry size 22	4
Stranded cotton	Evenweave 28 count	Tapestry size 24	3
Stranded cotton	Evenweave 32 count	Tapestry size 26	2–3
Kreinik blending filament	Aida 14 count	Tapestry size 24	3 + 1 strand blending filament
Kreinik blending filament	Aida 16 count	Tapestry size 26	2 + 1 strand blending filament
Kreinik blending filament	Aida 18 count	Tapestry size 28	1 + 1 strand blending filament

Hints & Techniques

Reading a chart

If the chart is too small to read easily, use a photocopier to enlarge it.

Be sure to read the instructions carefully before starting to make sure that you are using the correct number of threads and the correct fabric count. (Remember a design will come out larger if using a larger count and smaller if using a smaller count.)

Fabric

1. Iron the fabric before you start stitching to remove any creases (these will be impossible to remove afterwards).

2. Do not skimp on fabric; make sure that you leave a minimum of 7 cm (2 1/4 in) extra around your finished design to allow for framing or mounting.

3. Do not leave your fabric in a hoop after you have finished stitching; the longer it is in the hoop the more likely it is to leave a mark that is hard to remove.

4. Wash your hands regularly to prevent dirty marks on the fabric.

5. When using linen wash it in warm water and iron first to allow for shrinkage.

6. It is advisable to use a larger count when trying out dark fabrics for the first time, as it is easier to see the holes in the fabric. If you place a piece of white paper or cloth on your knee it will show through the holes so that you can stitch more easily.

7. To prevent your fabric from fraying, either edge it with masking tape or cut around the edge with pinking shears—this will be sufficient to prevent fraying.

Lighting

It is important to work in a good light, as this will prevent costly mistakes in your stitching and counting. Daylight is preferable but if working at night you can use a daylight lamp.

Stitching

1. Work all the cross stitch before adding backstitch outlines and highlights.

2. Do not work randomly around the chart; complete the embroidery in sections (line by line), completing one colour at a time in each section where possible so that you do not make mistakes in counting. For example, if you start with the border complete the whole border before moving on to another section, if you are stitching a pattern complete the pattern first. (See 'Reading a Cross Stitch Chart' on page 14 for more information.)

Hints & Techniques

3. Let your needle and thread dangle loosely at the back of the work occasionally to untwist the thread.

4. Snip your threads off neatly at the back when finished to avoid loose ends coming through to the front when stitching.

How to make counted work easier

If a design is complex and has a lot of fractional stitches (see page 18) you can outline it lightly on the fabric with a wash-out pen or soft pencil. (This will wash out afterwards.) Alternatively, you can outline the design first with a single strand of a lighter shade of thread. Once this is done you simply fill in the areas according to your chart.

How to calculate the size of your design

To work out how big a design will be when it is finished, simply divide the height and width in squares on the chart by the number of holes per inch (HPI) of your chosen fabric. If using linen or evenweave you will need to divide the HPI by 2 to give the number of stitches per inch.

Mistakes

Do not panic when you get a knot; quite often it will be just a loose knot that can be untangled by pulling the knot loop up to release it.

If you miscount, unpick your stitches slowly until you get back to where you were. If it is a large block snip the top arm of the cross stitches and unravel slowly.

Needles

Make sure you use the correct needle for the count of fabric, as it will slip through the holes easily. (See the Thread Usage Chart on page 10 .)

Change your needle often. If it becomes tarnished it will damage both fabric and threads.

Threads

1. Use a good quality recommended thread as it will remain colourfast and make all the difference to your finished work. Do not be tempted to use cheaper quality threads, as the colour will run.

2. Buy enough thread to complete your project as the dye lots vary and the second batch may not accurately match the first.

3. If you do run out of a thread colour take a reasonable-sized piece to your stockist so you can match it.

4. It is a good idea to store your threads in a bag while working to keep them free of dust and spillage. A clear plastic or cellophane bag is useful because you can see the thread colours when needed.

5. Do not mix threads from different brands, as the shades are never the same.

6. Use short lengths of thread, approximately 50 cm (20 in) or so, to prevent tangling. When using metallic or blending filaments use even shorter lengths, approximately 35 cm (18 in).

7. When ironing metallic threads make sure that the iron is not too hot and iron on the back only to prevent the thread melting.

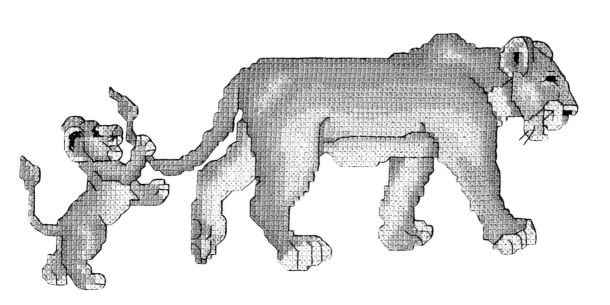

Stitch Instructions

Reading a cross stitch chart

A cross stitch design is worked from a chart which looks similar to a graph, made up of squares. Each square of the design has a symbol in it which represents a cross stitch. The squares on the chart represent the squares on the fabric (i.e. one block on Aida or one block on evenweave). It is usual to start from the centre of the chart so that the design is centred for mounting or framing, however I quite often find it easier to start from the top of the design

and work down, the reason being that it is easier to work a cross stitch beneath another cross stitch than it is to work above it. You can use a wash-out pen or soft pencil to mark the centre of your design and count up to the starting point so that you know exactly where the design will fit on the fabric.

The chart has a key next to it with all the symbols which relate to the thread colours. Where you see the symbol on the chart is where you stitch that particular colour on the fabric. The chart is generally made up of whole cross stitches, but many also have some fractional (three-quarter) stitches, and nearly all have backstitch outlines. There is more on this under Backstitch and Fractional Stitches.

Getting started

1. Find the centre of your fabric by folding it in half and then in half again. The centre of your chart is where the arrow lines intersect. Match the centre of your chart and the centre of your fabric. *NB Note* that the centre of a design with uneven numbers of stitches (e.g. 25 x 31) will fall on a square; the centre of a design with even numbers of stitches (e.g. 26 x 30) will fall in a hole.

2. You can choose whether or not to mount your fabric into a hoop to keep it taut.

3. Looking at the stranded cotton you will see that

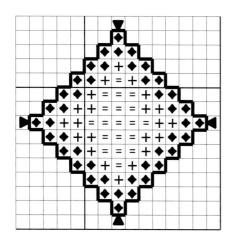

Cross stitch chart

		DMC
=	Pearl Grey	415
+	Steel Grey lt	318
◆	Black	310

Chart key

it has six strands. Pull out the number of strands specified in the instructions and thread them into the needle.

4. To start off either leave a small tail or a loop (see directions below).

5. Stitch the design (see directions for cross stitch on the various fabrics below), following the symbols on the chart.

How to begin and end cross stitch

Here are two ways to start off your cross stitch.

Tail method To do this you leave a length of thread at the back of your work; as you work along the row it will cover the thread. Hold your thread along the area to be stitched and secure it with the first few stitches.

Loop method To use this method you need to be working with one long strand of thread (instead of two of the usual length) folded in half. Put the two ends together and thread these through the needle leaving a loop at one end.

When you put the needle through on your second stitch catch it through the loop. This gives a nice neat finish.

Ending Pass the needle in and out of several stitches at the back of your work to secure, then cut the thread close to the fabric to give a neat finish.

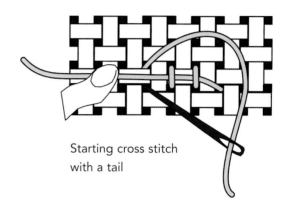

Starting cross stitch with a tail

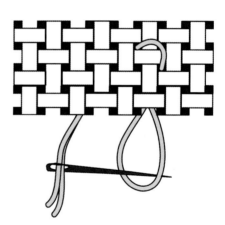

Starting cross stitch with a loop

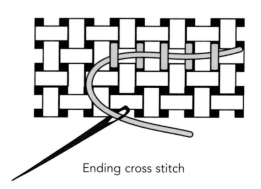

Ending cross stitch

Stitch Instructions

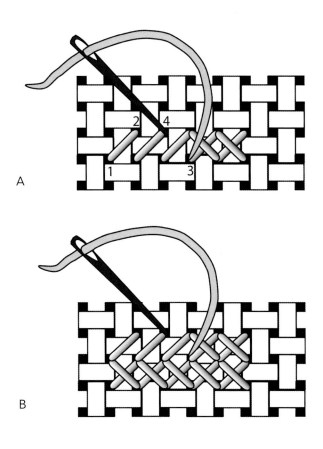

A

B

C

Basic cross stitch on Aida fabric

Aida fabric is woven into blocks and has a regular weave. Each cross stitch is stitched between the blocks, over four holes. This is the most popular type of fabric for cross stitching and is the most suitable for beginners. Aida fabric is available in different 'counts' or HPI, referring to the number of holes per inch; for example, 14 HPI gives you 14 cross stitches to each inch. The more holes per inch the smaller the cross stitches, that is, 18 HPI is very small and 8 HPI is very large. Aida is available in 18, 16, 14, 11 and 8 count.

A Each cross stitch is formed by making one diagonal stitch on top of another. To work a row of cross stitches bring your needle up at 1 and down at 2, repeating this first half of the cross stich across the row. To complete the cross stitch, bring the needle up at 3 and down at 4, repeating across the row. To form a single cross stitch bring the needle up at 1, down at 2, up at 3 and down at 4.

B Work the second and subsequent rows of cross stitches above the first row. Make sure that the top halves of the cross stitches all lie in the same direction, so that the stitches are even.

C Where possible work the cross stitches down but if you need to work cross stitches that go above each other, first make a full cross stitch (1) then make a half cross stitch above it (2), then make a full cross stitch above that (3), then come back to the previous stitch (2) and complete it. This method prevents you trying to go in and come out in the same hole twice, thus unravelling the stitch.

Cross stitch on evenweave or linen

Evenweave and linen fabric have a looser weave than Aida and are made up of woven single threads. Cross stitches are worked over two threads of the fabric across and two threads up (a nine-hole square) to form a block, whereas on Aida the stitch is worked over one block (four holes). The fabric is softer and finer than Aida but requires a little experience to work on successfully. Evenweave and

linen also come in different counts (HPI). It is much easier to do fractional stitches on evenweave.

Cross stitch on waste canvas

With waste canvas you can cross stitch a design on any fabric that does not have a grid, such as cotton, satin, etc. It can also be used to transfer a design onto items of clothing or blankets, sheets and towels. Waste canvas provides a grid for you to stitch on and has a blue line running down every fifth row of the fabric as a guide. Waste canvas also comes in different counts (HPI).

A Cut a piece of waste canvas the size of your design, plus approximately 5 cm (2 in) extra. Tack the piece to your chosen fabric or item. Stitch the

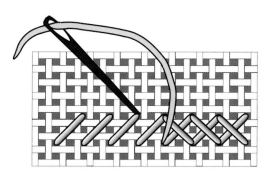

The cross stitch worked across two threads of the fabric across and two up (a nine-hole square).

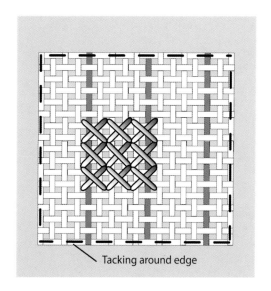

Tacking around edge

A

Stitch Instructions

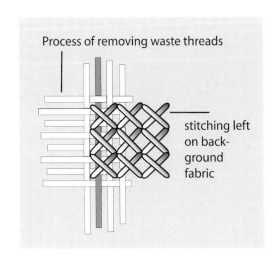

Process of removing waste threads

stitching left on back-ground fabric

B

design from your chart as usual, using the number of strands of thread specified. Stitch through both the waste canvas and background fabric.

B When all the stitching is complete trim away any excess waste canvas and remove the waste threads. You can soak it in water first, which removes the starch and softens the canvas, before you pull out each thread with a pair of tweezers. When all waste canvas threads have been removed you will be left with just the design on the background fabric.

Fractional stitches

Fractional stitches are half or three-quarter stitches, used to replace a full cross stitch so that the shape is followed more closely. A half stitch is shown as a smaller version of the cross stitch symbol on the chart and is worked over half of the square. A three-quarter stitch is worked over half a square as shown below. A three-quarter stitch can be worked over two squares across or up to closely follow the outline as shown below. When working a fractional stitch on Aida you will have to pierce the centre of the square, but with evenweave the holes are already there in the nine-hole square.

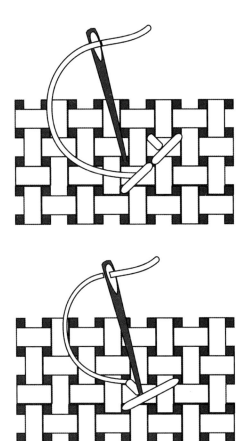

Backstitch

Backstitch is used to outline parts of the design or to add details. The backstitch areas are identified by the heavy black lines that go through or around the symbols. One strand of cotton is used for backstitch unless otherwise specified.

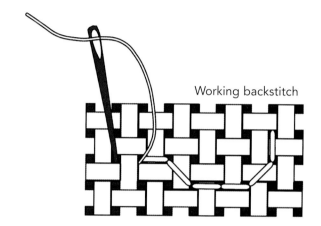

Working backstitch

French knot

A Bring the thread up at 1. Hold the thread between thumb and forefinger as illustrated. Loop the thread over the needle twice. The number of loops depends on how big you require the knot to be, but two loops are usual.

B Insert the needle into the fabric at 1, close to the original hole but not in the same hole.

C Pull the loop taut to form the knot.

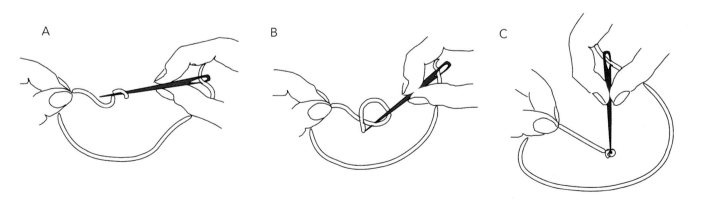

A   B   C

Finishing Instructions

You can frame your cross-stitch,
or apply it to many items such as
pillow cases, blankets, clothing,
notebooks or spectacle cases.

Washing and finishing your work

When your stitching is complete you can wash it in cool water and gently press it dry on the back after laying it face down on several folds of fluffy towel. If you are working with linen always pre-wash it in case it shrinks.

There are many ways to use finished work:

• **Frame it** (you can take it to a professional framer or do it yourself). If you frame it yourself you will need to stretch it (see following instructions), but a professional framer will stretch it for you as part of the job.

• **Make up your design** into a pillowcase, cushion cover, table cloth, table mat, table napkin, hand towel, make-up bag, wash bag, linen bag, undies bag, bookmark, pencil case or spectacle case.

• **Use waste canvas to transfer your design** to a sweatshirt, knitted pullover, shirt or T-shirt, baby items, a blanket, sheet, pillowcase or towel.

• **Purchase ready-made items** such as crystal bowls, notebooks, glass containers, coasters, plastic mugs, plastic rulers, spectacle cases and greeting cards, and decorate with cross stitch motifs.

Stretching completed work for framing

Wash the completed stitching in cool water and iron on the wrong side. Cut a piece of mounting board to fit your design plus about 2.5 cm (1 in) extra around the edge to allow for mounting when framing. There are various mountboards available, some with wadding and some without. (Self-adhesive mountboard does not require stretching and is much easier to use; see below.)

A Centre the mountboard on the back of the design. Fold the fabric over and push pins through the fabric and board along one edge.

B Stretching the fabric gently, pull it across to the opposite side, fold over and pin. Starting from one end, lace the fabric from one end to the other, crossing the threads.

C Now pin and lace the other two sides in the same way. Fold in and slipstitch the corners. Once all four sides are laced, remove the pins. The work should be fairly taut and even, and is ready to be framed.

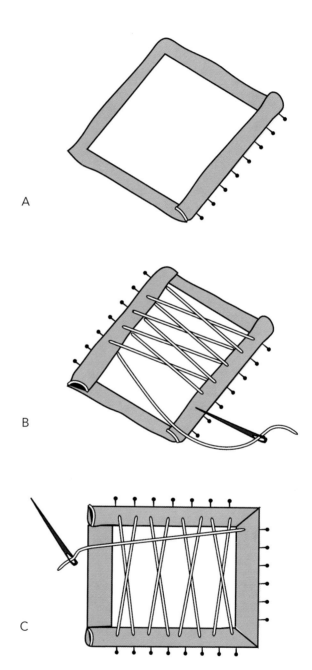

A

B

C

Finishing Instructions

Mounting finished stitching onto card without stretching

Take a piece of self-adhesive mounting board at least 2.5 cm (1 in) larger all round than the finished design. There are two ways to make an attractive mount with this.

The simplest method is trim the fabric to within 2 cm (³/₄ in) of the edges of the design and apply it directly to the adhesive mounting board, smoothing and straightening the fabric as you go.

The other way is to take a piece of lightweight card in a matching or contrasting colour to your stitched piece and cut it to the size of the adhesive mount. Apply this piece of card to the mount. Trim the fabric to within about 1 cm (³/₈ in) of the edges of the design. You can fray a few lines to give it character. Apply fabric glue to the edges of the design and a little in the centre and, using a piece of clean white paper, smooth the glue evenly over the back of the design. Apply the design to the centre of the card so that it is framed by the coloured mount.

Making a greeting card

Various types of greeting card blanks are available in a range of sizes, some with three folds, some with two, with different shaped apertures. The diagram shows a three-fold card with a square aperture, as used in the first four designs.

1. Make sure that the cross stitch design you have chosen fits the aperture on the card (or vice versa).

2. Complete the cross stitch design and position it behind the aperture for the best effect.

3. Make pencil marks on the back of the fabric as a guide, and cut to the required size.

4. Secure the fabric to the back of the central panel with double-sided tape or a little craft glue. Make sure it's facing the right way up.

5. Fold the inner panel back over the design and secure with double-sided tape or a little craft glue.

You can make your own two-fold greeting card with no aperture using medium weight card in any colour or texture. Cut the card to double the width of the card that you want—for example, for a greeting card 10 cm (4 in) square, cut a strip of card 10 cm (4 in) wide and 20 cm (8 in) long, using a very sharp craft knife against a metal rule or straight-edge to keep the cuts straight. For a three-fold card 10 cm (4 in) square with an aperture, cut a strip 10 cm (4 in) wide and 30 cm (12 in) long, and mark and cut an aperture of the required size in the centre panel. It is helpful to make cards in sizes that can fit into purchased envelopes.

Making a greeting card

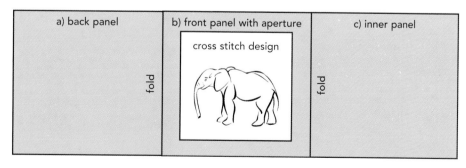

Finishing Instructions

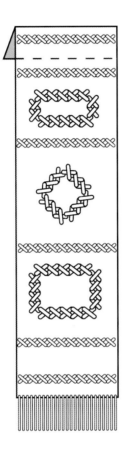

Making a bookmark

Aida ribbon fabric 16 count, 5 cm wide x 25 cm long (2 x 10 in) is used for the bookmarks in this book.

1. Start the stitching at the top end of the chart. Turn under the top end of the ribbon about 5 rows down and stitch the first row of the design through both thicknesses.

2. When all the stitching is complete fray the bottom edge to within 2 rows of the last row of stitching.

3. Wash the bookmark in cool water and iron on the back of the work.

4. Place a piece of iron-on interfacing cut to the size of the bookmark over the back of the work. Iron into place. (Alternatively you can sew a piece of matching cotton fabric to the back with small hemming stitches.)

5. Secure a tassel or backstitch a name or greeting at the bottom end if desired.

Making a pincushion

Trim away any excess fabric from the finished work to within about 1 cm (³/₈ in) of the edge of the design. Cut a piece of backing fabric to the same size and pin or tack it to the front piece, with right sides facing. Sew three sides together, leaving the fourth side open. Turn inside out and fill with stuffing, then stitch up the gap to complete. You can add some braid around the edge by slipstitching it into place.

Making a scissors-keeper or potpourri sachet

These are made in the same way as a pincushion but are very much smaller. To complete the scissors-keeper attach some braid to one corner of the small cushion and make a loop, thread the loop through one handle of the scissors then pass the scissors through the loop. A potpourri sachet is just a smaller version of the pincushion stuffed with potpourri.

Finishing Instructions

Making a spectacle case

You will need a piece of Aida fabric (or fabric of your choice) approximately 25 cm (10 in) square, a piece of felt approximately 22 cm (9 in) square and about 60 cm (24 in) of cord.

Cut a piece of fabric 22 cm (9 in) square. Calculate the finished size of your design according to the count used. (Remember, if using 14 count the design will be larger than on 16 count.) Work a running stitch about 2 cm (³/₄ in) in from the edges as a guide (this will be removed later). Centre the design within this.

When all the stitching is complete fold the two sides together with right sides facing. Backstitch a seam along the long edge and down one end. Turn the open edges under and iron in place. Make a felt pouch for the lining. Cut a square of felt slightly smaller than the outer case, fold in half, stitch along the long side and one end, and turn inside out. Fit it inside the spectacle case (it will be slightly shorter) and slipstitch the open edges of the pouch to the turned-in folds of the outer case. Slipstitch the cord around the open end of the case, down one long side, across the bottom and up the other long side to finish off.

Making a spectacle case

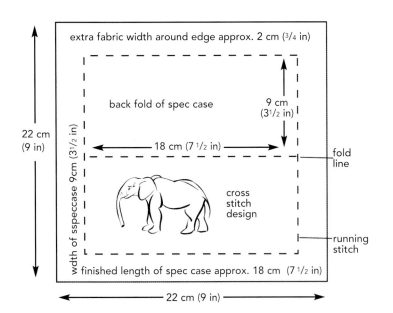

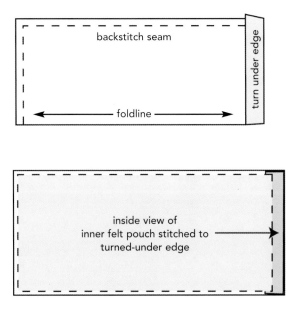

Making a pencil case

You will need a piece of Aida fabric (or fabric of your choice) 28 x 22 cm (11 x 9 in), a piece of felt approximately 28 x 22 cm (11 x 9 in), a piece of Velcro 8 cm (3 in) long and a piece of cord approximately 80 cm (32 in) long. Cut a piece of fabric 28 x 22 cm (11 x 9 in). Calculate the finished size of your design according to the count used. (Remember, if using 14 count the design will be larger than on 16 count.) Work a running stitch about 2 cm ($^3/_4$ in) in from the edges as a guide (this will be removed later). Centre the design within one half of this area, using the fold line as the guide to the base.

When all the stitching is complete fold the two sides together with right sides facing. Backstitch a seam along each short side, leaving the long side open. Turn the extra allowance under on the two edges and iron in place.

Make a felt pouch for the lining slightly smaller than the pencil case, sew up the two short sides and turn inside out. Fit it into the pencil case and slipstitch the open edges to the turned-in folds of the outer casing. Take an 8 cm (3 in) piece of Velcro and sew or glue into the centre of the opening. Finally take a piece of cord and slipstitch it up one end of the pencil case, around the opening and down the other end to finish it off.

Making a pencil case

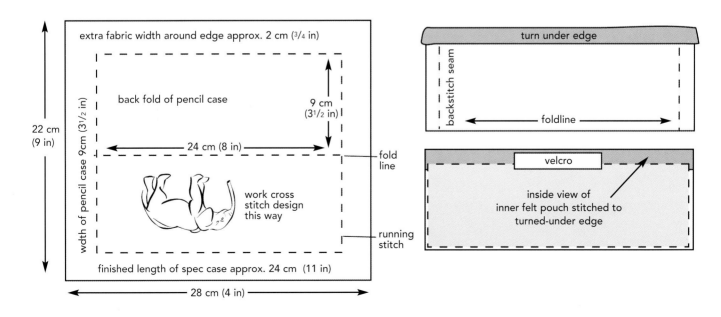

FINISHING INSTRUCTIONS **27**

General Instructions for

1. Find the centre of your fabric by folding it in half and then in half again; mark the centre square with a pencil mark. (See 'Getting Started' in Stitch Instructions for further information.)

2. If a design measures 25 x 25 squares, for example, count up from the centre square 12 squares to give you the top of your design and across from the centre square 12 squares to give you the left side of your design. Do the same down and to the right. Draw in pencil lines at the corners where the lines meet at right angles.

3. If you are right-handed, begin stitching at the top left-hand side of the chart and work across and down. If you are left-handed, start at the top right-hand corner and work across and down.

4. Cut a piece of stranded cotton about 50 cm (20 in) long in the colour indicated on the key for this point on the chart. You will see that there are 6 strands—pull out the number of strands specified in the design instructions and thread into the needle specified.

Working a Design

5. To start off leave a small tail of thread at the back of the fabric and work this tail under your stitches as you go along. If using 2 strands of thread you can use the loop method which is much tidier.

6. Each symbol on the chart represents a single cross stitch and its position is counted on the fabric using the chart as a guide. Stitch all the cross stitch, changing colours as needed as you work across each row.

7. Some symbols on the charts ask for three-quarter stitches; where these occur, follow the directions for fractional stitches.

8. When all the cross stitch is complete outline the design in backstitch using the needle specified, usually in black thread but sometimes in other colours as specified in the design instructions. At this point you will also add any lettering or other design elements required. Your stitching is complete.

9. Wash your work in cool water and while still damp iron face down on a fluffy towel until dry.

10. Mount in a greeting card or otherwise finish as specified in the instructions.

Detailed instructions are included for the Starter Project. For all other projects, only special instructions relevant to the particular project are noted.

Starter Project

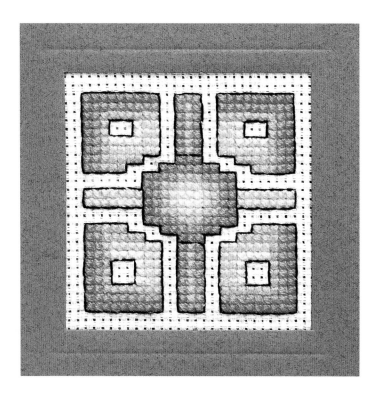

This is a simple project

aimed to get you started. If you are unfamiliar with cross stitch techniques, read the sections Materials and Equipment, Hints and Techniques, and Stitch Instructions first, then simply follow the instructions below.

Instructions

This design has been stitched on 14 count Aida fabric using 3 strands of thread in a size 24 needle for cross stitch and 1 strand in a size 26 needle for backstitch.

1. Find the centre of your fabric by folding it in half and then in half again, mark the centre square with a pencil mark.

2. The design measures 25 x 25 squares so count up from the centre square 12 squares (to give you the top of your design) and down 12 squares to give the bottom of the design. Count across from the centre square 12 squares to give you the left side of your design, and the same to give you the right side. Draw pencil lines at corners where the lines meet.

3. If you are right-handed, begin stitching at the top left-hand side of the chart and work across and down. If you are left-handed, start at the top right-hand corner and work across and down.

4. Cut a piece of stranded cotton about 50 cm (20 in) long in the colour indicated in the key for this point on the chart. You will see that there are 6 strands—pull out 3 strands and thread into your size 24 needle.

5. To start off leave a small tail of thread at the back of the fabric and work this tail under your stitches as you go along.

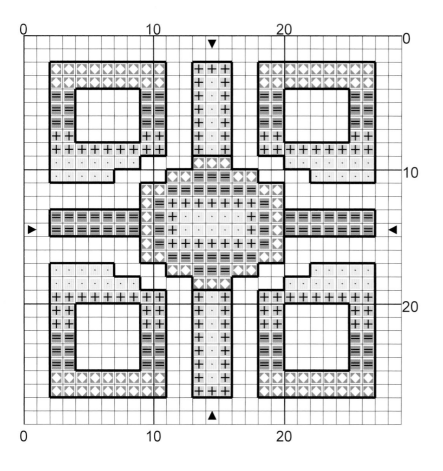

You will need

- Stranded cotton as per key
- Tapestry needles
  size 24 (cross stitch)
  size 26 (backstitch)
- Aida 14 count
  15 cm (6 in) square
- Greeting card with
  5.5 cm (2 in) square aperture

Design size

- 25 x 25 stitches
  11 count = 5.8 cm (2.3 in) square
  14 count = 4.5 cm (1.8 in) square
  18 count = 3.5 cm (1.4 in) square

6. Each symbol on the chart represents a single cross stitch and its position is counted on the fabric using the chart as a guide. Stitch all the cross stitch, changing colours as needed.

7. When all the stitching is complete thread one strand of black thread in a size 26 needle and outline the cross stitching in backstitch. Your stitching is complete.

8. Wash finished embroidery in cool water and while still damp iron face down on a fluffy towel until dry.

		DMC	Anchor	Madeira
▬	Pale Terracotta	3854	883	2302
◇	Terracotta	3853	324	0310
·	Yellow ultra vy lt	3823	386	0111
✛	Peach	3855	8	2309

9. Mount in the greeting card as explained in the finishing section.

You are now ready to go on to the other projects in this book.

Sunlight Card

Send a bit of cheery, sparkling sunshine to someone and light up their day! This simple greeting card can be used for any occasion. You can make your own card or use a purchased one.

Sunlight Card special special notes

If you need any reminders, refer to General Instructions for Working a Design on page 28.

This design has been stitched on 14 count Aida fabric using 3 strands of thread for cross stitch. The sun is stitched with 2 strands of cotton + 1 strand of blending filament.

Backstitching is done in black using 1 strand, or gold using 2 strands.

Some symbols on the chart ask for three-quarter stitches; follow directions for fractional stitches.

Work the eight-pointed stars in one strand of gold metallic thread as indicated by solid black lines on the chart. Work from the centre of the star and make four straight stitches, one square up, down, left and right. Work four more straight stitches at angles between the first four to complete.

Wash finished embroidery in cool water and iron face down on a fluffy towel.

Mount finished work in the greeting card as directed in the finishing instructions.

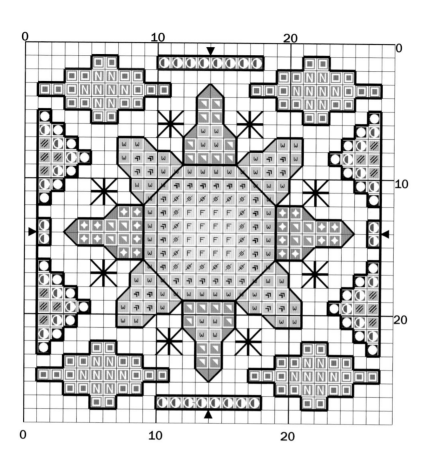

		DMC	Anchor	Madeira	Kreinik
W	Tangerine lt	742	303	0107	027
◣	Tangerine med	741	314	0201	027
✦	Tangerine dk	740	316	0202	027
F	Yellow vy lt	745	300	0111	028
⌀	Yellow lt	744	301	0110	028
⌐	Yellow med	743	305	0113	028
▦	Baby Blue lt	159	130	1014	
◖	Navy Blue med dk	336	149	1007	
◑	Navy Blue vy lt	161	137	0911	
▣	Orange vy dk	606	334	0209	
N	Orange dk	608	330	0207	

You will need

- Stranded cotton and

metallic thread as per key

- Gold metallic thread (DMC No 5282)
- Tapestry needles

size 24 (cross stitch)

size 26 (backstitch)

- Aida 14 count 15 cm (6 in) square
- Greeting card with 5.5 cm (2 in) square aperture

Design size

- 26 x 26 stitches

11 count = 6 cm (2.4 in) square

14 count = 4.7 cm (1.9 in) square

18 count = 3.7 cm (1.4 in) square

Twilight Card

This design depicts twilight,

which is the time just after sunset or just before sunrise. Typically the landscape is bathed in the golden light of the moon and stars twinkle against a backdrop of a smoky blue sky. The card can be used for any occasion and the alphabet at the back of the book can be used to insert names or dates as desired.

Twilight Card special notes

If you need any reminders, refer to General Instructions for Working a Design on page 28.

This design has been stitched on 14 count Aida fabric using 3 strands of thread in the size 24 needle for cross stitch. The moon is stitched using a blend of 2 strands cotton (yellow beige lt) + 1 strand gold metallic. All backstitching is done either in black or gold in the size 26 needle using 2 strands for emphasis. Follow directions for fractional stitches where needed.

Work the eight-pointed stars in one strand of gold metallic thread as indicated by solid black lines on the chart. Work from the centre of the star and make four straight stitches, one square up, down, left and right. Work four more straight stitches at angles between the first four to complete.

Wash finished embroidery in cool water and iron face down on a fluffy towel.

Use a purchased card or make one of your own. Cut around the edge of the design leaving a border of about 10 rows. Fray the first few rows. Using fabric glue, stick the design onto the centre of the card.

		DMC	Anchor	Madeira
☐	Black	310	403	Black
◤	Golden Brown vy lt	3827	363	2301
✦	Golden Brown med	976	308	2302
⊓	Golden Brown med dk	3826	1049	2306
▽	Gold	783	307	2211
◇	Topaz	728	291	0107
◪	Topaz med	782	901	2212
I	Yellow Beige med	3046	887	2206
▬	Topaz vy dk	780	365	2214
▪	Yellow Beige lt	3047	886	2205
Ɛ	Metallic Gold	5282	278	2206

You will need

- Stranded cotton and metallic gold as per key
- Tapestry needles

size 24 (cross stitch)

size 26 (backstitch)

- Aida 14 count

15 cm (6 in) square in dark smoky blue

- Two-fold card approx 13 x 15 cm (5 x 6 in)

Design size

- 41 x 31 stitches

11 count = 9.5 x 7.2 cm (3.7 x 2.8 in)

14 count = 7.4 x 5.6 cm 2.9 x 2.2 in)

18 count = 5.8 x 4.4 cm (2.3 x 1.7 in)

Welcome Card

The word mauya (pronounced ma-oo-ya) means 'welcome'. The sun is a symbol of warmth and cheer. This card can be used to welcome someone to your home, to welcome a new baby or for any other occasion. Use the alphabet chart at the back of the book so that you can place the appropriate wording, names or dates as desired.

Welcome Card special notes

If you need any reminders, refer to General Instructions for Working a Design on page 28.

This design has been stitched on 14 count Aida fabric using 3 strands of thread in a size 24 needle or 1 strand of thread in a size 26 needle for backstitch The sun has been stitched using a blend of 2 strands of thread + 1 strand of Kreinik metallic as indicated on the key. Other colours such as mauve lt, mauve and electric blue med are blended with Kreinik metallic as per the key. The four corner swirls and the centre diamonds are outlined in metallic silver using 1 strand. Some symbols on the chart ask for three-quarter stitches; follow directions for fractional stitches.

Wash finished embroidery in cool water and iron face down on a fluffy towel.

To assemble the design in the card, cut around the edge of the design leaving a one-row border. Cut a piece of hessian 10 cm (4 in) square and fray the first couple of strands. Either use a purchased two-fold card or make your own. Using fabric glue, stick the design on to the hessian, then the hessian + design to the centre of the card. Place a heavy book on top and allow to dry for at least an hour.

If hessian is not readily available you can use an oatmeal or similar colour evenweave or rough weave fabric.

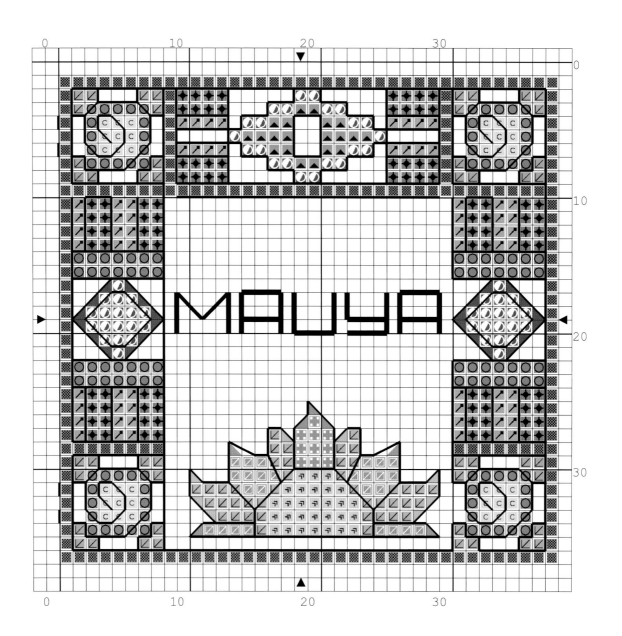

You will need

- Stranded cotton and metallic thread as per key
- Blending filament
- Tapestry needles
size 24 (cross stitch)
size 26 (backstitch)
- Aida 14 count
15 cm (6 in) square
- Two-fold card
approx. 14 cm (5.5 in) square
- Hessian 1
3 cm (5 in) square

Design size

- 38 x 36 stitches
11 count = 8.8 x 8.3 cm (3.5 x 3.3 in)
14 count = 6.9 x 6.5 cm (2.7 x 2.6 in)
18 count = 5.4 x 5.1 cm (2.1 x 2 in)

		DMC	Anchor	Madeira	Kreinik
◤	Tangerine lt	742	303	0107	
⌐	Yellow med	743	305	0113	028
◿	Tangerine dk	740	316	0202	027
⊞	Tangerine med	741	314	0201	127
◖	Lavender ultra dark	3837	99	2709	
◥	Mauve lt med	3608	86	0709	007HL
●	Blue Violet	340	118	0902	
◆	Mauve	3607	87	0708	024
▓	Electric Blue med	996	433	1103	006
C	Blue Violet vy lt	3747	117	0907	
▲	Lavender dk	209	109	0803	

Congratulations

Sampler

This is a small sampler that can be used to commemorate a wedding, engagement, anniversary, birth of a baby, birthday, success in exams, promotion, passing a driving test or any other occasion. The word makorokoto means 'congratulations' or 'well done'. Taking out the line below it will give you space to add a name and date using the alphabet at the back of the book.

Congratulations Sampler special notes

If you need any reminders, refer to General Instructions for Working a Design on page 28.

This design has been stitched on 14 count Aida fabric using 3 strands of thread or 2 strands thread + 1 strand metallic in a size 24 needle for cross stitch, and 1 strand in a size 26 needle for backstitch.

All backstitching is indicated in a heavy black line (indicating black using 1 strand) or a heavy red line (indicating metallic copper using 1 strand). The backstitching for the wording is done using 2 strands of black.

When all the cross stitching is complete thread a size 26 needle with 1 strand of black (or copper) and outline areas as indicated.

Work the eight-pointed stars in one strand of gold metallic thread as indicated by solid black lines on the chart. Work from the centre of the star and make four straight stitches, one square up, down, left and right. Work four more straight stitches at angles between the first four to complete.

Wash finished embroidery in cool water and iron face down on a fluffy towel. Mount as desired

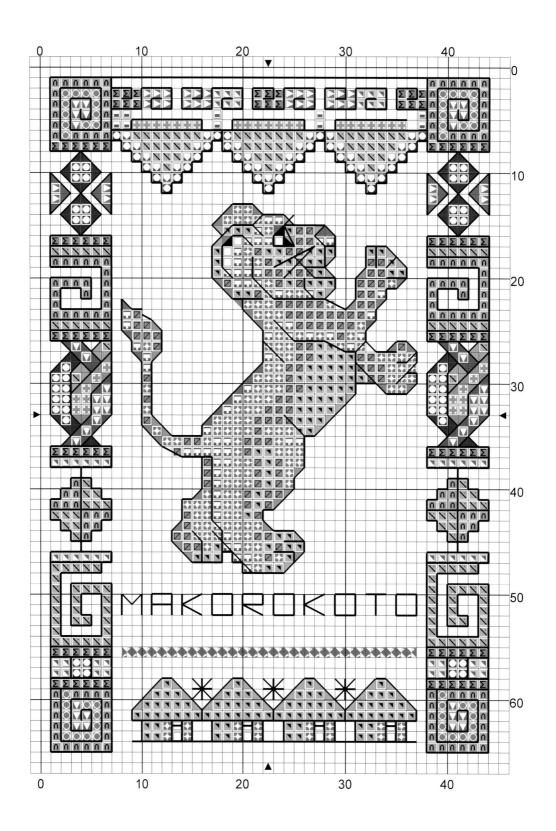

You will need

• Stranded cotton and
metallic thread as per key
• Blending filament
• Tapestry needles
size 24 (cross stitch)
size 26 (backstitch)
• Aida 14 count
18 x 22 cm (7 x 9 in)

Design size

• 44 x 64 stitches
11 count = 10.2 x 14.8 cm (4 x 5.8 in)
14 count = 8 x 11.6 cm (3.1 x 4.6 in)
18 count = 6.2 x 9 cm (2.4 x 3.6 in)

		DMC	Anchor	Madeira
	Delft	809	130	0909
	Delft dk	798	137	0911
	Royal Blue med	797	147	0912
	Chartreuse bright	704	256	1308
	Chartreuse	703	238	1307
	Christmas Green lt	702	226	1306
	Forest Green lt	907	255	1410
	Golden Brown vy lt	3827	363	2301
	Golden Brown lt	977	1002	2307
	Golden Brown med	976	308	2302
	Golden Brown med dk	3826	1049	2306
	Black	310	403	Black
	Bright Turquoise lt	3846	1089	1103
	Bright Turquoise	3845	1089	1110
	Bright Turquoise	3844	410	1110
	Copper	5279	9046	0210

Welcome Sampler

This is a small sampler that can be used to commemorate the birth of a baby, welcome to our home, welcome to our country or any other occasion, simply by changing the wording. The word mauya means 'welcome'. You can add in your own wording, names, dates, etc. by using the alphabet chart at the back of the book.

The area between the bird and the sun has been left free for you to place your lettering and the finished photograph is just an example of the placing. Take out the lines on either side of the wording on the chart to make extra room.

Welcome Sampler special notes

If you need any reminders, refer to General Instructions for Working a Design on page 28.

This design has been stitched on 14 count Aida fabric using 3 strands of thread in a size 24 needle for cross stitch, and 1 strand in a size 26 needle for backstitch. Where a Kreinik metallic equivalent is given on the key this indicates a blending of 2 strands of thread + 1 strand of metallic for cross stitch.

All backstitching is done in black using 1 strand.

Wash finished embroidery in cool water and iron face down on a fluffy towel. Mount as desired.

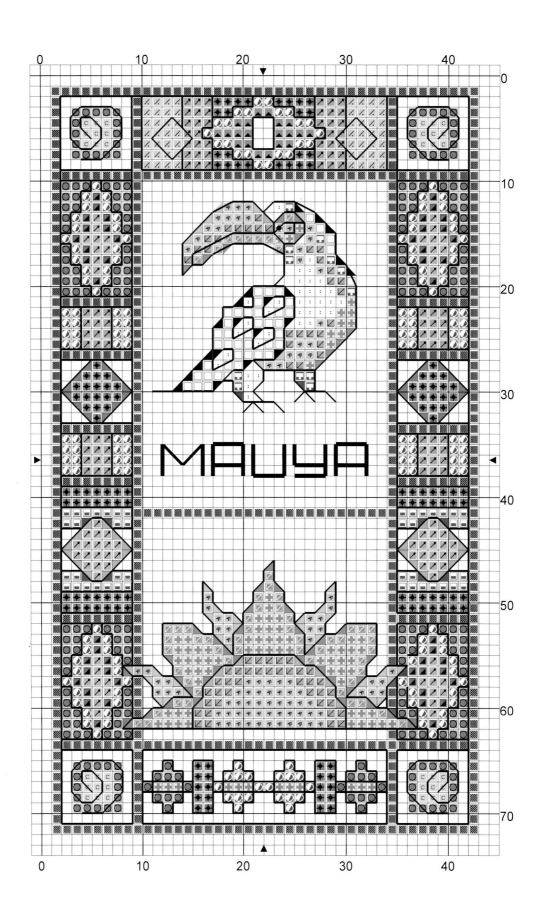

You will need

- Stranded cotton and metallic thread as per key
- Tapestry needles size 24 (cross stitch) size 26 (backstitch)
- Aida 14 count 18 x 23 cm (7 x 9 in)

Design size

- 42 x 71 stitches

11 count = 9.7 x 16.4 cm (3.8 x 6.5 in)

14 count = 7.6 x 12.9 cm (3 x 5.1 in)

18 count = 5.9 x 10 cm (2.3 x 3.9 in)

		DMC	Anchor	Madeira	Kreinik
	Black	310	403	Black	
	Yellow med	743	305	0113	028
	Tangerine lt	742	303	0107	
	Winter White	3865	2	White	032
	Tangerine dk	740	316	0202	027
	Tangerine med	741	314	0201	127
	Steel Grey dk	414	235	1801	
	Lavender med	210	108	0802	
	Lavender dk	209	109	0803	
	Lavender vy dk	208	111	0804	
	Lavender ultra dark	3837	99	2709	
	Blue Violet	340	118	0902	
	Blue Violet med	3746	1030	0903	
C	Blue Violet vy lt	3747	117	0907	
	Mauve vy lt	3609	85	0710	092
	Mauve lt med	3608	86	0709	007HL
	Mauve	3607	87	0708	024
	Electric Blue med	996	433	1103	006

Young Rhino Bookmark

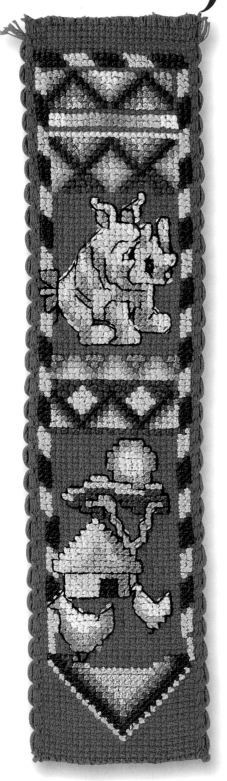

Traditionally, Zimbabwean children are given an animal totem at birth. The rhino totem would generally be given to a person of some strength. This design can also be used to make a picture if stitched on a larger count fabric such as 14 or 11 count.

Young Rhino Bookmark special notes

If you need any reminders, refer to General Instructions for Working a Design on page 28.

This design has been stitched on 16 count Aida ribbon fabric using 3 strands of thread in a size 24 needle for cross stitch and 1 strand in a size 26 needle for backstitch.

Start the bookmark at the top end of the chart. Turn under the top end of your Aida ribbon about 5 rows down and stitch the first row through both thicknesses.

Wash finished embroidery in cool water and iron face down on a fluffy towel.

Complete the bookmark as directed in the finishing instructions section.

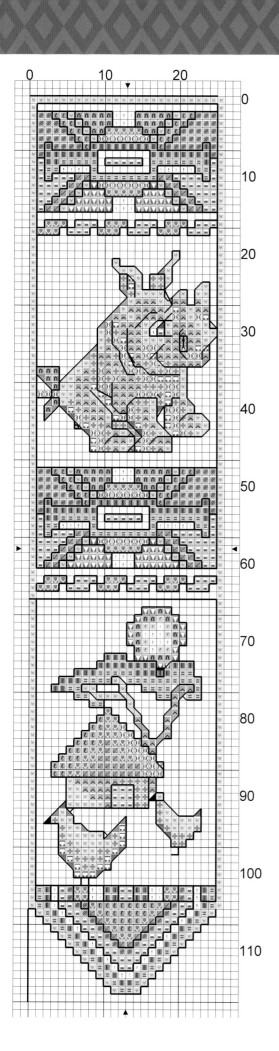

You will need

- Stranded cotton as per key
- Tapestry needles size 24 (cross stitch) size 26 (backstitch)
- Aida ribbon 16 count 25 cm (10 in) long

Design size

- 26 x 117 stitches

11 count =
6 x 27 cm (2.4 x 10.6 in)

14 count =
4.7 x 21.2 cm (1.9 x 8.4 in)

16 count =
4.1 x 18.6 cm (1.6 x 7.3 in)

		DMC	Anchor	Madeira
▬	Wedgwood med dk	6760	1039	1106
∩	Chartreuse bright	704	256	1308
◢	Very Dark Straw	3852	306	0114
▼	Antique Gold dk	3820	306	2209
!	White bright	B5200	1	White
ℓ	Antique Gold lt	3822	305	0109
⊓	Old Gold vy dk	3829	901	2212
⋙	Old Gold vy lt	677	886	2207
⋀	Old Gold lt	676	891	2208
✚	Old Gold med	729	890	2012
◑	Old Gold dk	680	907	2210
☐	Black	310	403	Black
‖	Turquoise lt	959	185	1113
▤	Teal Green	3848	205	1202
▽	Christmas Green lt	702	226	1306
⫽	Wedgwood lt	519	1038	1105
f	Laurel Green vy lt	772	1043	1604

Young Ostrich Bookmark

The word for ostrich is mhou. It can be a vicious attacker when threatened. Traditionally ostrich eggs are highly prized for ritual purposes. This design can also be used to make a picture if stitched on a larger count such as 14 or 11.

Young Ostrich Bookmark special notes

If you need any reminders, refer to General Instructions for Working a Design on page 28.

This design has been stitched on 16 count Aida ribbon fabric using 3 strands of thread in a size 24 needle for cross stitch and 1 strand in a size 26 needle for backstitch.

Start the bookmark at the top end of the chart. Turn under the top end of your Aida ribbon about 5 rows down and stitch the first row through both thicknesses.

Wash finished embroidery in cool water and iron face down on a fluffy towel.

Make up the bookmark as directed in the finishing instructions section.

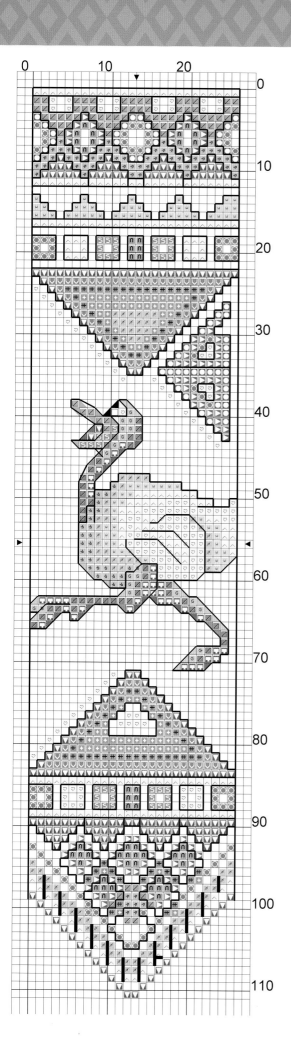

You will need

- Stranded cotton as per key
- Tapestry needles
size 24 (cross stitch)
size 26 (backstitch)
- Aida ribbon 16 count
25 cm (10 in) long

Design size

- 26 x 111 stitches

11 count =

6 x 25.6 cm (2.4 x 10.1 in)

14 count =

4.7 x 20.1 cm (1.9 x 7.9 in)

16 count =

4.1 x 17.6 cm (1.6 x 6.9 in)

		DMC	Anchor	Madeira
✦	Burnt Orange lt	972	298	0107
╫	Burnt Orange med dk	971	316	0204
▽	Orange Red med	947	330	0205
▼	Orange Red dk	900	332	0208
∩	Chartreuse bright	704	256	1308
●	Chartreuse	703	238	1307
◖	Christmas Green med	701	227	1305
▷	Christmas Green lt	702	226	1306
⌐	Yellow med	743	305	0113
◣	Tangerine lt	742	303	0107
S	Tangerine dk	740	316	0202
♡	White	Blanc	1	White
⌃	Off White	746	386	0101
w	Yellow vy lt	745	300	0111
⌀	Yellow lt	744	301	0110
⌐	Yellow med	743	305	0113
G	Autumn Gold lt	3855	301	2309
◪	Golden Brown lt	977	1002	2307
⊔	Golden Brown med dk	3826	1049	2306
☐	Black	310	403	Black

Young Warthog Bookmark

The warthog is known as ngiri. A person with this totem is said to be easily provoked and extremely cheeky! This design can also be used to make a picture if stitched on a larger count fabric such as 14 or 11 count.

Young Warthog Bookmark special notes

If you need any reminders, refer to General Instructions for Working a Design on page 28.

This design has been stitched on 16 count Aida ribbon fabric using 3 strands of thread in a size 24 needle for cross stitch and 1 strand in a size 26 needle for backstitch.

Start the bookmark at the top end of the chart. Turn under the top end of your Aida ribbon about 5 rows down and stitch the first row through both thicknesses.

Wash finished embroidery in cool water and iron face down on a fluffy towel.

Complete the bookmark as directed in the finishing instructions section.

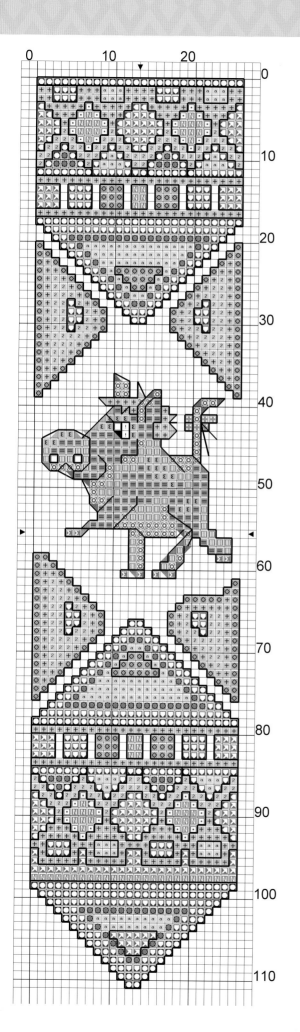

You will need

- Stranded cotton as per key
- Tapestry needles
size 24 (cross stitch)
size 26 (backstitch)
- Aida ribbon 16 count
25 cm (10 in) long

Design size

- 26 x 111 stitches

11 count =

6 x 25.6 cm (2.4 x 10.1 in)

14 count =

4.7 x 20.1 cm (1.9 x 7.9 in)

16 count =

4.1 x 17.6 cm (1.6 x 6.9 in)

		DMC	Anchor	Madeira
a	Baby Blue vy lt	775	975	1001
	Baby Blue med lt	3755	140	1013
	Navy lt	312	147	1005
	Navy Blue med dk	336	149	1007
N	Chartreuse	703	238	1307
	Christmas Green lt	702	226	1306
	Christmas Green med	701	227	1305
	Christmas Green dk	699	923	1303
2	Topaz vy lt	727	293	0110
+	Topaz lt	726	297	0109
◇	Topaz	725	305	0106
	Chartreuse bright	704	256	1308
!	White bright	B5200	1	White
Ɛ	Golden brown vy lt	3827	363	2301
=	Golden Brown lt	977	1002	2307
◉	Golden Brown med dk	3826	1049	2306
‖‖	Golden Brown med	976	308	2302
Σ	Beige Brown lt	841	378	1911
□	Black	310	403	Black

Chameleon Bookmark

The chameleon is generally harmless but it is commonly believed that if you are bitten by a chameleon it will not let go until you apply snuff to its lips. This design can also be used to make a picture if stitched on a larger count fabric such as 14 or 11 count.

Chameleon Bookmark special notes

If you need any reminders, refer to General Instructions for Working a Design on page 28.

This design has been stitched on 16 count Aida ribbon fabric using 3 strands of thread in a size 24 needle for cross stitch and 1 strand in a size 26 needle for backstitch.

Start the bookmark at the top end of the chart. Turn under the top end of your Aida ribbon about 5 rows down and stitch the first row through both thicknesses.

Wash finished embroidery in cool water and iron face down on a fluffy towel.

Complete the bookmark as directed in the finishing instructions section.

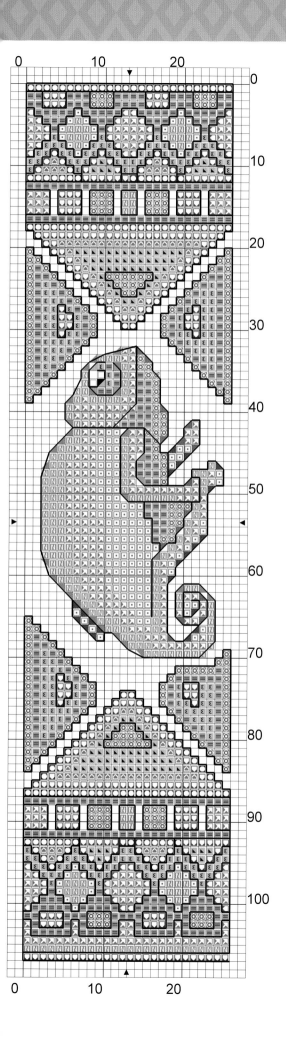

You will need

- Stranded cotton as per key
- Tapestry needles
  size 24 (cross stitch)
  size 26 (backstitch)
- Aida ribbon 16 count
  25 cm (10 in) long

Design size

- 26 x 107 stitches

11 count =

6 x 24.7 cm (2.4 x 9.7 in)

14 count =

4.7 x 19.4 cm (1.9 x 7.6 in)

16 count =

4.1 x 17 cm (1.6 x 6.7 in)

		DMC	Anchor	Madeira
◣	Blue Violet lt	341	117	0901
⬠	Cornflower Blue med	793	176	0906
▽	Cornflower Blue dk	792	177	0905
◯	Cornflower Blue vy dk	791	123	0904
N	Chartreuse	703	238	1307
▷	Christmas Green lt	702	226	1306
▫	Christmas Green med	701	227	1305
◁	Christmas Green dk	699	923	1303
ε	Golden Brown vy lt	3827	363	2301
=	Golden brown lt	977	1002	2307
◉	Golden Brown med dk	3826	1049	2306
□	Black	310	403	Black

Fish Eagle Bookmark

It is thought that to dream of fish or fishing means wealth or progress. The sun symbolises the 'light in your life', and the word chiyedza means 'progress and light'. The Fish Eagle is commonly found at Kariba Dam, the largest man-made lake in the world. This design can also be used to make a picture if stitched on a larger count fabric such as 14 or 11 count.

Fish Eagle Bookmark special notes

If you need any reminders, refer to General Instructions for Working a Design on page 28.

This design has been stitched on 16 count Aida ribbon fabric using 3 strands of thread in a size 24 needle for cross stitch and 1 strand in a size 26 needle for backstitch.

Start the bookmark at the top end of the chart. Turn under the top end of your Aida ribbon about 5 rows down and stitch the first row through both thicknesses.

Wash finished embroidery in cool water and iron face down on a fluffy towel. Complete the bookmark as directed in the finishing instructions section.

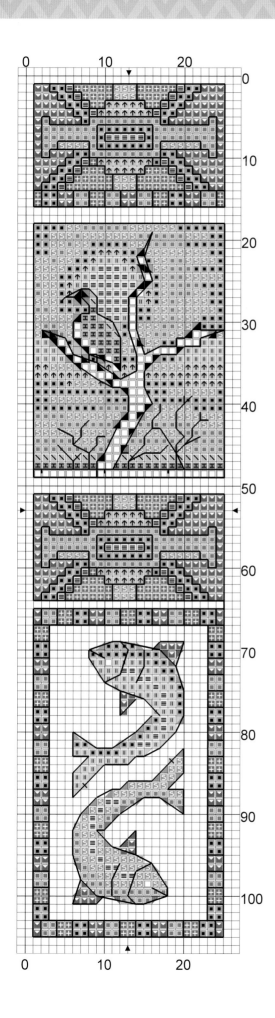

You will need

- Stranded cotton as per key
- Tapestry needles

size 24 (cross stitch)

size 26 (backstitch)

- Aida ribbon 16 count

25 cm (10 in) long

Design size

24 x 104 stitches

11 count = 5.5 x 24 cm (2.2 x 9.5 in)

14 count = 4.4 x 18.9 cm (1.7 x 7.4 in)

16 count = 3.8 x 16.5 cm (1.5 x 6.5 in)

		DMC	Anchor	Madeira
▣	Christmas Red lt	3801	46	0411
▽	Navy Blue med dk	336	149	1007
✚	Pistachio Green ultra dk	890	1044	1314
■	Gold	783	307	2211
≡	Golden Yellow vy lt	3078	292	0102
‖	Topaz lt	726	297	0109
↑	Topaz	725	305	0106
S	Orange Spice med	721	324	0308
◣	Steel Grey dk	414	235	1801
⊥	Pewter Grey vy dk	3799	236	1713
⊓	Black	310	403	Black

Big Five Bookmark

The totems of the big five—rhino, leopard, buffalo, lion and elephant—are believed to confer strong personalities on those who bear them. This design can also be used to make a picture if stitched on a larger count fabric such as 14 or 11 count.

Big Five Bookmark special notes

If you need any reminders, refer to General Instructions for Working a Design on page 28.

This design has been stitched on 16 count Aida ribbon fabric using 3 strands of thread in a size 24 needle for cross stitch and 1 strand in a size 26 needle for backstitch.

Start the bookmark at the top end of the chart. Turn under the top end of your Aida ribbon about 5 rows down and stitch the first row through both thicknesses.

Wash finished embroidery in cool water and iron face down on a fluffy towel.

Complete the bookmark as directed in the finishing instructions section.

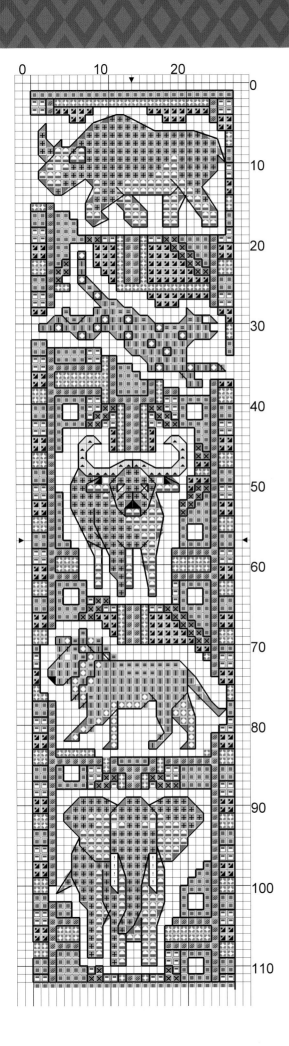

You will need

- Stranded cotton as per key
- Tapestry needles

size 24 (cross stitch)

size 26 (backstitch)

- Aida ribbon

16 count 25 cm (10 in) long

Design size

- 26 x 112 stitches

11 count =

6 x 25.9 cm (2.4 x 10.2 in)

14 count =

4.7 x 20.3 cm (1.9 x 8 in)

16 count =

4.1 x 17.8 cm (1.6 x 7 in)

		DMC	Anchor	Madeira
▣	Christmas Red lt	3801	46	0411
➕	Cornflower Blue med	793	176	0906
✕	Cornflower Blue med dk	3807	122	0905
◠	Cornflower Blue dk	792	177	0905
▭	Cornflower Blue vy dk	791	123	0904
▨	Leaf Green med	992	186	1202
◆	Leaf Green vy dk	991	189	1204
❘	Gold	783	307	2211
=	Topaz	725	305	0106
◪	Golden Brown vy lt	3827	363	2301
◇	Golden Brown med dk	3826	1049	2306
!	White bright	B5200	1	White
▲	Pearl Grey	415	398	1802
☐	Black	310	403	Black

Woman with Basket Bookmark

Traditionally a woman who maintains the family unit, which comprises children, parents and grandparents, is given the name Musha Mukadzi, meaning 'the woman is the heart of the home'. This design can also be used to make a picture if stitched on a larger count fabric such as 14 or 11 count.

Woman with Basket Bookmark special notes

If you need any reminders, refer to General Instructions for Working a Design on page 28.

This design has been stitched on 16 count Aida ribbon fabric using 3 strands of thread in a size 24 needle for cross stitch and 1 strand in a size 26 needle for backstitch.

Start the bookmark at the top end of the chart. Turn under the top end of your Aida ribbon about 5 rows down and stitch the first row through both thicknesses.

Wash finished embroidery in cool water and iron face down on a fluffy towel.

Complete the bookmark as directed in the finishing instructions section.

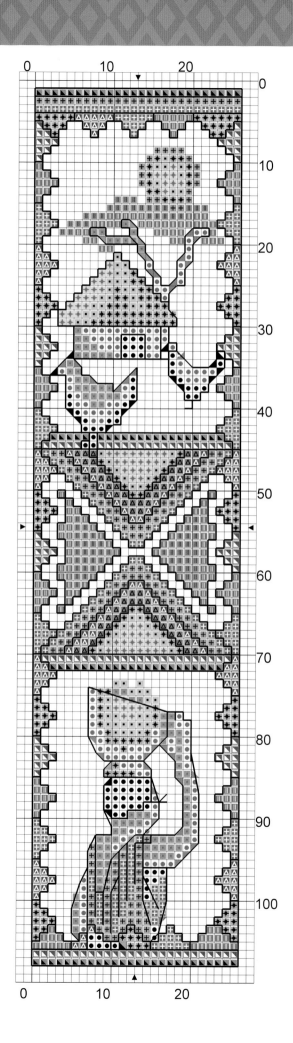

You will need

- Stranded cotton as per key
- Tapestry needles
size 24 (cross stitch)
size 26 (backstitch)
- Aida ribbon 16 count
25 cm (10 in) long

Design size

- 26 x 107 stitches
11 count =
6 x 24.7 cm (2.4 x 9.7 in)
14 count =
4.7 x 19.4 cm (1.4 x 5.9 in)
16 count =
4.1 x 17 cm (1.6 x 6.7 in)

		DMC	Anchor	Madeira
	Melon med	3706	33	0409
	Christmas Red lt	3801	46	0411
	Blue Violet	340	118	0902
	Blue Violet med	3746	1030	0903
	Antique Blue med	931	1034	1711
	Antique Blue vy dk	3750	1036	1007
	Turquoise lt	959	185	1113
	Turquoise vy dk	943	188	1203
	Gold	783	307	2211
	Topaz lt	726	297	0109
	Topaz	725	305	0106
	Beige Brown med	840	379	1912
	Beige Brown vy dk	838	381	2003
	Black	310	403	Black

Kudu & Cheetah Bookmark

The kudu is much sought after for its meat but also revered for its grace and splendour. The cheetah possesses qualities of swiftness and beauty. This design can also be used to make a picture if stitched on a larger count fabric such as 14 or 11 count.

Kudu & Cheetah Bookmark special notes

If you need any reminders, refer to General Instructions for Working a Design on page 28.

This design has been stitched on 16 count Aida ribbon fabric using 3 strands of thread in the size 24 needle for cross stitch and 1 strand in the size 26 needle for backstitch.

Start the bookmark at the top end of the chart. Turn under the top end of your Aida ribbon about 5 rows down and stitch the first row through both thicknesses.

Wash finished embroidery in cool water and iron face down on a fluffy towel.

Complete the bookmark as directed in the finishing instructions section.

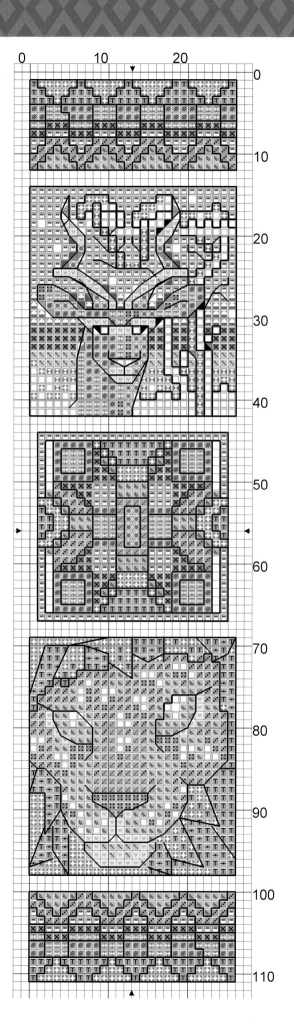

You will need

- Stranded cotton as per key
- Tapestry needles
size 24 (cross stitch)
size 26 (backstitch)
- Aida ribbon 16 count
25 cm (10 in) long

Design size

- 26 x 110 stitches
11 count =
6 x 25.4 cm (2.4 x 10 in)
14 count =
4.7 x 20 cm (1.9 x 7.9 in)
16 count =
4.1 x 17.5 cm (1.6 x 6.9 in)

		DMC	Anchor	Madeira
✖	Cornflower Blue med dk	3807	122	0905
	Cornflower Blue dk	792	177	0905
	Cornflower Blue vy dk	791	123	0904
	Chartreuse bright	704	256	1308
T	Christmas Green lt	702	226	1306
✦	Christmas Green dk	699	923	1303
	Gold	783	307	2211
◣	Topaz	725	305	0106
▨	Golden Brown vy lt	3827	363	2301
▦	Golden Brown med dk	3826	1049	2306
◩	Beige Brown med	840	379	1912
▩	Beige Brown dk	839	1050	1913
◉	Beige Brown vy dk	838	381	2003
⌄	Pearl Grey	415	398	1802
◥	Steel grey dk	414	235	1801
✕	Pewter Grey dk	413	236	1713
▢	Black	310	403	Black

Guineafowl Bookmark

The guineafowl or hanga is thought to be a spirit medium. To come across a guineafowl is considered good luck; if war is imminent the sighting of a guineafowl could mean peace. This design can also be used to make a picture if stitched on a larger count fabric such as 14 or 11 count.

Guineafowl Bookmark special notes

If you need any reminders, refer to General Instructions for Working a Design on page 28.

This design has been stitched on 16 count Aida ribbon fabric using 3 strands of thread in the size 24 needle for cross stitch and 1 strand in the size 26 needle for backstitch.

Start the bookmark at the top end of the chart. Turn under the top end of your Aida ribbon about 5 rows down and stitch the first row through both thicknesses.

Wash finished embroidery in cool water and iron face down on a fluffy towel.

Complete the bookmark as directed in the finishing instructions section.

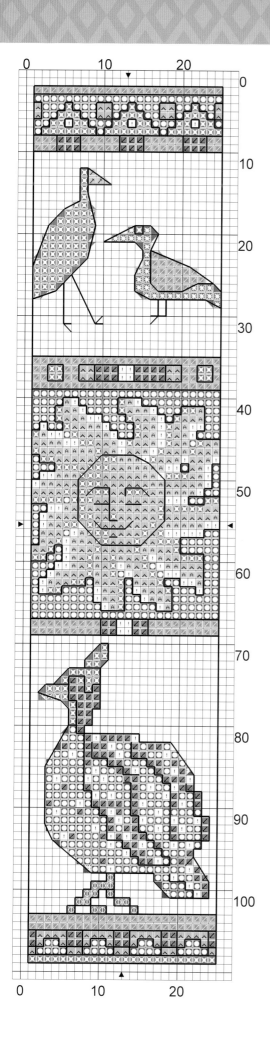

You will need

- Stranded cotton as per key
- Tapestry needles
size 24 (cross stitch)
size 26 (backstitch)
- Aida ribbon 16 count
25 cm (10 in) long

Design size

- 24 x 107 stitches
11 count =
5.5 x 24.7 cm (2.2 x 9.7 in)
14 count =
4.4 x 19.4 cm (1.7 x 7.6 in)
16 count =
3.8 x 17 cm (1.5 x 6.7 in)

		DMC	Anchor	Madeira
	Coral red	891	29	0411
	Blue Violet med	3746	1030	0903
	Antique Blue lt	932	343	1710
	Antique Blue vy dk	3750	1036	1007
	Chartreuse	703	238	1307
A	Topaz vy lt	727	293	0110
	Topaz lt	726	297	0109
	Topaz	725	305	0106
	Brown lt	434	310	2009
!	White bright	B5200	1	White

Giraffe & Rhinoceros Bookmark

The Zimbabwean name for the giraffe is twiza and for the rhino is chipembere. It is traditionally beleived thatan angry god planted the boabab tree upside down, thus accounting for the stout trunks which are able to store water and the root like branches. Trees with diameters of over 10m may be over 2000 years old. This design can also be used to make a picture if stitched on a larger count fabric such as 14 or 11 count.

Giraffe & Rhinoceros Bookmark special notes

If you need any reminders, refer to General Instructions for Working a Design on page 28.

This design has been stitched on 16 count Aida ribbon fabric using 3 strands of thread in the size 24 needle for cross stitch and 1 strand in the size 26 needle for backstitch.

Start the bookmark at the top end of the chart. Turn under the top end of your Aida ribbon about 5 rows down and stitch the first row through both thicknesses.

Wash finished embroidery in cool water and iron face down on a fluffy towel.

Complete the bookmark as directed in the finishing instructions section.

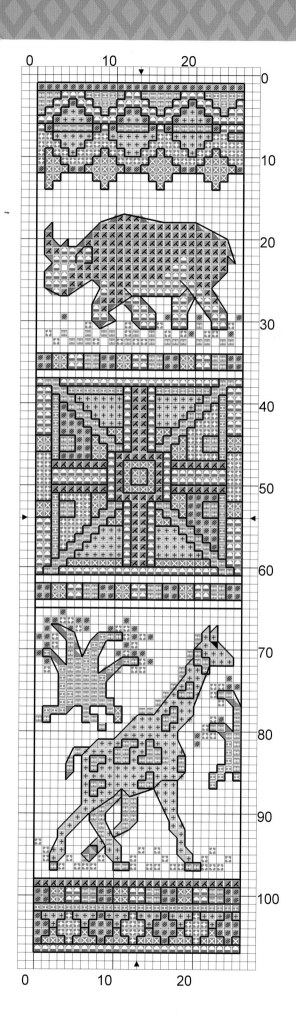

You will need

- Stranded cotton as per key
- Tapestry needles size 24 (cross stitch) size 26 (backstitch)
- Aida ribbon 16 count 25 cm (10 in) long

Design size

- 26 x 106 stitches

11 count =

6 x 24.5 cm (2.4 x 9.6 in)

14 count =

4.7 x 19.2 cm (1.9 x 7.6 in)

16 count =

4.1 x 16.8 cm (1.6 x 6.6 in)

		DMC	Anchor	Madeira
◤	Cornflower Blue med	793	176	0906
◠	Cornflower Blue dk	792	177	0905
▦	Leaf Green med	992	186	1202
◆	Leaf Green vy dk	991	189	1204
⊥	Copper lt	921	1003	0311
✕	Red Copper	919	340	0313
+	Golden Brown vy lt	3827	363	2301
▥	Golden-Brown med dk	3826	1049	2306
☐	Black	310	403	Black

Hippo & Waterfall Bookmark

The hippo or bvuu is commonly found wallowing in the Zambezi River, which flows over the Victoria Falls, one of the natural wonders of the world. The Falls' Zimbabwean name, mosi oa tunya, means 'smoke that thunders'. This design can also be used to make a picture if stitched on a larger count fabric such as 14 or 11 count.

Hippo & Waterfall Bookmark special notes

If you need any reminders, refer to General Instructions for Working a Design on page 28.

This design has been stitched on 16 count Aida ribbon fabric using 3 strands of thread in the size 24 needle for cross stitch and 1 strand in the size 26 needle for backstitch.

Start the bookmark at the top end of the chart. Turn under the top end of your Aida ribbon about 5 rows down and stitch the first row through both thicknesses.

Wash finished embroidery in cool water and iron face down on a fluffy towel.Complete the bookmark as directed in the finishing instructions section.

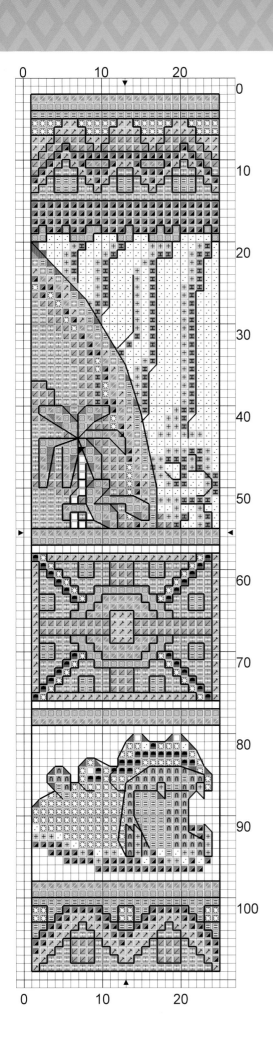

You will need

- Stranded cotton as per key
- Tapestry needles
size 24 (cross stitch)
size 26 (backstitch)
- Aida ribbon 16 count
25 cm (10 in) long

Design size

- 24 x 107 stitches
11 count =
5.5 x 24.7 cm (2.2 x 9.7 in)
14 count =
4.4 x 19.4 cm (1.7 x 7.6 in)
16 count =
3.8 x 17 cm (1.5 x 6.7 in)

		DMC	Anchor	Madeira
⋒	Pink lt	893	40	0413
⊟	Pink dk	891	29	0411
◖	Blue Violet lt	341	117	0901
✳	Blue Violet med	3746	1030	0903
◣	Electric Blue med	996	433	1103
◢	Chartreuse	703	238	1307
▨	Christmas Green med	701	227	1305
⌁	Topaz lt	726	297	0109
⊞	Tangerine med	741	314	0201
◿	Golden brown lt	977	1002	2307
⊞	Golden brown med dk	3826	1049	2306
⸫	White	Blanc	1	White
+	Pearl grey dk	414	235	1801
Ⅱ	Steel Grey dk	414	235	1801
☐	Black	310	403	Black

Ostrich Family Outing

The flightless ostrich, known as mhou, is the largest living bird and the fastest animal on two legs. The ostrich inhabits dry open plains and semi-desert and, fascinatingly, makes a growling sound similar to a lion's growl. This design can be used to make up a spectacle case, pencil case or any other suitable item of your choice. See finishing instructions for ideas.

Ostrich Family Outing special notes

If you need any reminders, refer to General Instructions for Working a Design on page 28.

This design has been stitched on 18 count Aida fabric using 2 strands of thread in a size 26 needle for cross stitch and 1 strand in a size 28 needle for backstitch, and made up into a spectacle case.

Wash finished embroidery in cool water and iron face down on a fluffy towel.

Complete the spectacle case or item of your choice as directed in the finishing instructions.

You will need

- Stranded cotton as per key
- Tapestry needles
size 26 (cross stitch)
size 28 (backstitch)
- Aida fabric 18 count
20 x 30 cm (9 x 12 in)
30 cm (12 in) square for spectacle case

Design size

- 69 x 134 stitches
11 count = 30.9 x 15.9 cm (12.2 x 6.3 in)
14 count = 24.3 x 12.5 cm (9.6 x 4.9 in)
18 count = 18.9 x 9.7 cm (7.4 x 3.8 in)

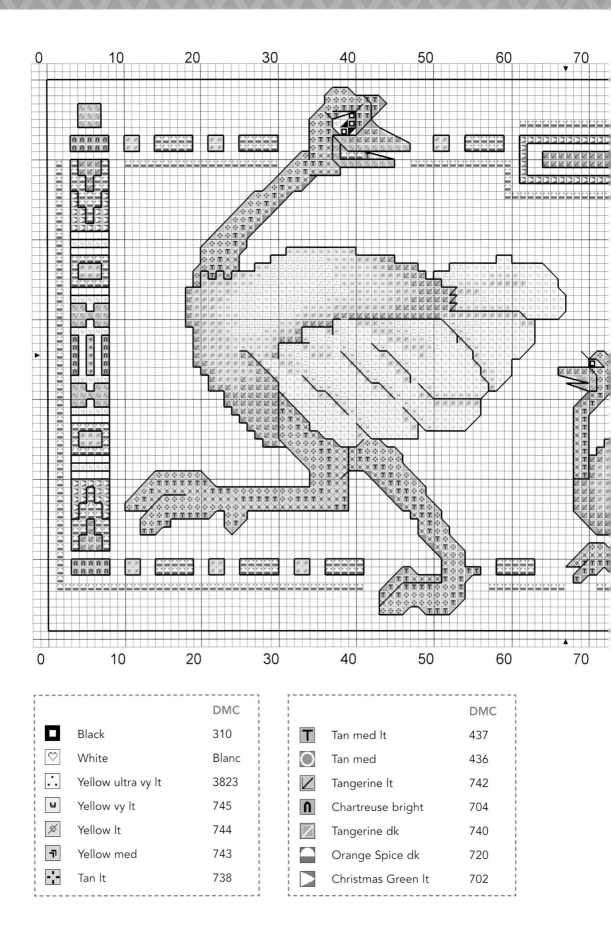

		DMC				DMC
◻	Black	310	T	Tan med lt	437
♡	White	Blanc	○	Tan med	436
∴	Yellow ultra vy lt	3823	╱	Tangerine lt	742
w	Yellow vy lt	745	∩	Chartreuse bright	704
⊘	Yellow lt	744	◺	Tangerine dk	740
⅂	Yellow med	743	◡	Orange Spice dk	720
⁘	Tan lt	738	▷	Christmas Green lt	702

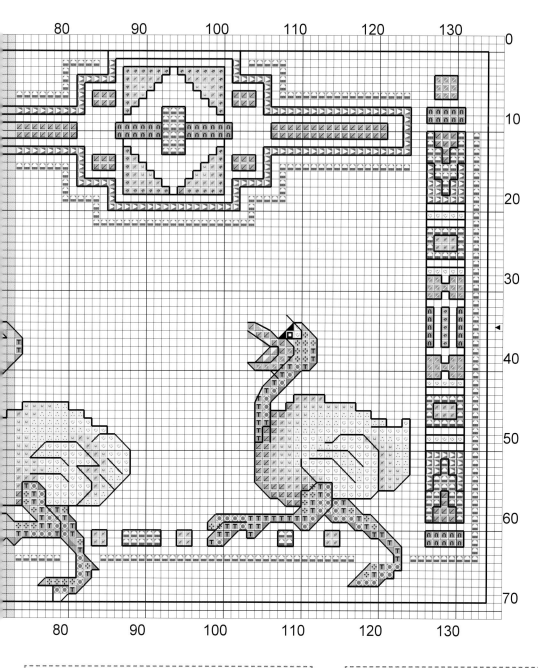

		Anchor	Madeira
■	Black	403	Black
♡	White	1	White
⠒	Yellow ultra vy lt	386	0111
w	Yellow vy lt	300	0111
⊠	Yellow lt	301	0110
↰	Yellow med	305	0113
⠶	Tan lt	942	2013

		Anchor	Madeira
T	Tan med lt	362	2012
●	Tan med	1045	2011
◪	Tangerine lt	303	0107
∩	Chartreuse bright	256	1308
◪	Tangerine dk	316	0202
◖	Orange Spice dk	326	0309
▷	Christmas Green lt	226	1306

Rhino Family Outing

Although the black rhino or chipembere is believed to be aggressive, its behaviour is due to the fact that it has poor eyesight combined with very acute hearing and smell. When it senses a foreign presence its reaction is a mock charge to frighten off the intruder. Because of its poor eyesight it sometimes runs in the wrong direction. This design can be used to make up a spectacle case, pencil case or any other suitable item of your choice. See finishing instructions for ideas.

Rhino Family Outing special notes

If you need any reminders, refer to General Instructions for Working a Design on page 28.

This design has been stitched on 18 count Aida fabric using 2 strands of thread in a size 26 needle for cross stitch and 1 strand in a size 28 needle for backstitch, and made up into a spectacle case.

Wash finished embroidery in cool water and iron face down on a fluffy towel.

Complete the spectacle case or item of your choice as directed in the finishing instructions.

You will need

- Stranded cotton as per key
- Tapestry needles
size 26 (cross stitch)
size 28 (backstitch)
- Aida fabric 18 count
18 x 24 cm (7 x 9.5 in)
28 cm (11 in) square for spectacle case

Design size

- 97 x 54 stitches
11 count = 22.4 x 12.5 cm (8.8 x 4.9 in)
14 count = 17.6 x 9.8 cm (6.9 x 3.9 in)
18 count = 13.7 x 7.6 cm (5.4 x 3 in)

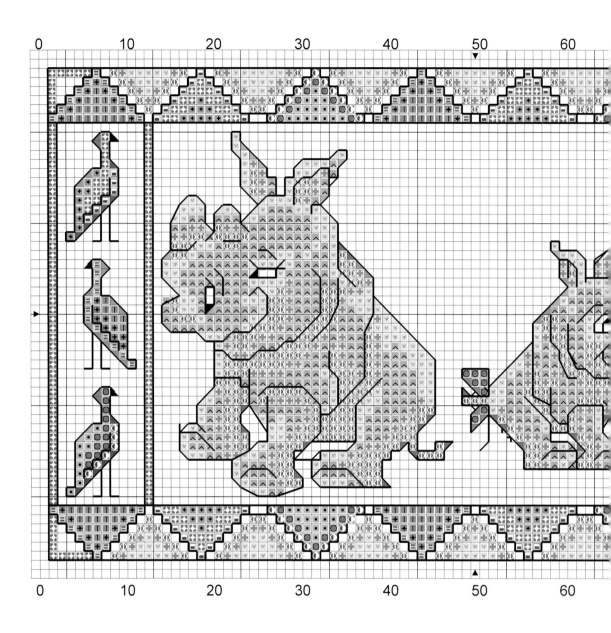

		DMC				DMC
■	Baby Blue Pale	3841	✦	Copper vy lt		922
◐	Baby Blue med lt	3755	▭	Copper med		920
◐	Navy Blue vy lt	322	⌄	Old Gold vy lt		677
↑	Blue Green lt	589	▲	Old Gold lt		676
✚	Teal Green lt	3849	✚	Old Gold med		729
▤	Teal Green	3848	◑	Old Gold dk		680
✦	Mahogany vy lt	402	☐	Black		310

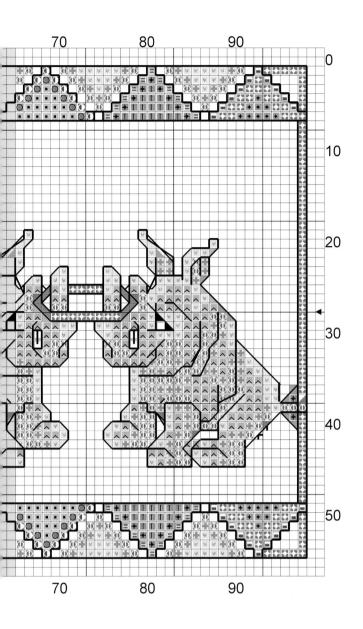

		Anchor	Madeira
■	Baby Blue Pale	1096	1001
◖	Baby Blue med lt	140	1013
◑	Navy Blue vy lt	978	1004
↑	Blue Green lt	167	1111
✛	Teal Green lt	849	2508
▤	Teal Green	205	1202
✦	Mahogany vy lt	1047	2307

		Anchor	Madeira
✧	Copper vy lt	1003	031
▭	Copper med	1004	0312
⩔	Old Gold vy lt	886	2207
⋀	Old Gold lt	891	2208
▦	Old Gold med	890	2012
◑	Old Gold dk	907	2210
☐	Black	403	Black

Warthog Family Outing

The endearing little hoglets are comical to watch as a whole family trots off in single file with their tails held straight up. The adult warthogs run with their tails vertical so that they are visible to their young in the long grass. This design can be used to make up a spectacle case, pencil case or any other item you choose. See finishing instructions for ideas.

Warthog Family Outing special notes

If you need any reminders, refer to General Instructions for Working a Design on page 28.

This design has been stitched on 18 count Aida fabric using 2 strands of thread in a size 26 needle for cross stitch and 1 strand in a size 28 needle for backstitch, and made up into a spectacle case.

Wash finished embroidery in cool water and iron face down on a fluffy towel.

Complete the spectacle case or item of your choice as directed in the finishing instructions section.

You will need

- Stranded cotton as per key
- Tapestry needles
size 26 (cross stitch)
size 28 (backstitch)
- Aida fabric 18 count
19 x 26 cm (7.5 x 10 in)
29 cm (11.5 in) square for spectacle case

Design size

- 118 x 61 stitches
11 count = 27.2 x 14.1 cm (10.7 x 5.5 in)
14 count = 21.4 x 11.1 cm (8.4 x 4.4 in)
18 count = 16.7 x 8.6 cm (6.6 x 3.4 in)

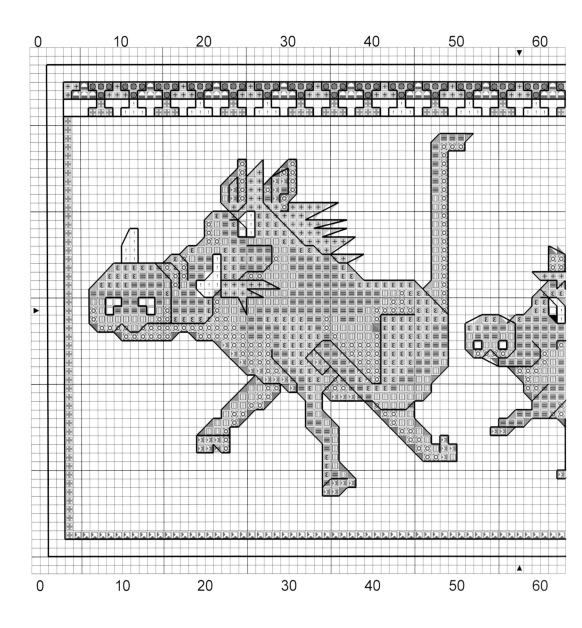

		DMC				DMC
⊓	Christmas Red lt	3801		▥	Golden Brown med	976
◉	Blue Violet	340		◉	Golden Brown med dk	3826
⊞	Chartreuse bright	704		!	White bright	B5200
⊠	Christmas Green lt	702		⊠	Beige Brown lt	841
ε	Golden Brown vy lt	3827		+	Topaz lt	726
=	Golden Brown lt	977		☐	Black	310

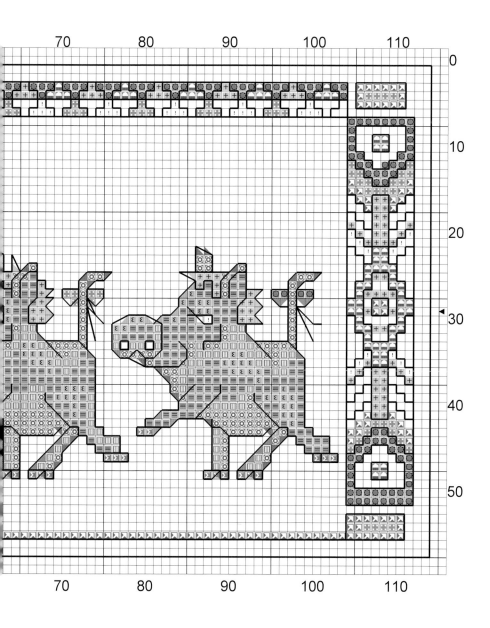

		Anchor	Madeira
	Christmas Red lt	46	0411
	Blue Violet	118	0902
	Chartreuse bright	256	1308
	Christmas Green lt	226	1306
	Golden Brown vy lt	363	2301
	Golden Brown lt	1002	2307

		Anchor	Madeira
	Golden Brown med	308	2302
	Golden Brown med dk	1049	2306
	White bright	1	White
	Beige Brown lt	378	1911
	Topaz lt	297	0109
	Black	403	Black

Lion Family Outing

A lioness produces one to six cubs in a litter, the average being two or three. Like all cats they are helpless when born, and their eyes remain closed for about three weeks. When the lioness goes out to hunt, she leaves the young cubs behind in thick brush. When the cubs are old enough to fend for themselves they accompany their mother, but for some time are placed well out of harm's way while the actual hunt is taking place. This design can be used to make up a spectacle case, pencil case or any other suitable item of your choice. See finishing instructions for ideas.

Lion Family Outing special notes

If you need any reminders, refer to General Instructions for Working a Design on page 28.

This design has been stitched on 18 count Aida fabric using 2 strands of thread in a size 26 needle for cross stitch and 1 strand in a size 28 needle for backstitch, and made up into a spectacle case.

Wash finished embroidery in cool water and iron face down on a fluffy towel.

Make up into spectacle case or other chosen item as directed in the finishing instructions section.

You will need

• Stranded cotton as per key

Tapestry needles

size 26 (cross stitch)

size 28 (backstitch)

Aida fabric 18 count

19 x 26 cm (7.5 x 10 in)

29 cm (11.5 in) square for spectacle case

Design size

•150 x 77 stitches

11 count = 34.6 x 17.8 cm (13.6 x 7 in)

14 count = 27.2 x 14 cm (10.7 x 5.5 in)

18 count = 21.2 x 10.9 cm (8.3 x 4.3 in)

		DMC			DMC
∧	Cream	712	▽	Green med	987
T	Tan med lt	437	.	Off White	746
◇	Tan vy lt	739	♡	White	Blanc
◆	Pistachio Green vy lt	369	G	Autumn Gold lt	3855
●	Tan med	436	✦	Autumn Gold dk	3853
▤	Brown vy lt	435	⊘	Yellow lt	744
∨	Pistachio Green lt	368	⁄	Autumn Gold	38545
☐	Black	310	⅂	Yellow med	743

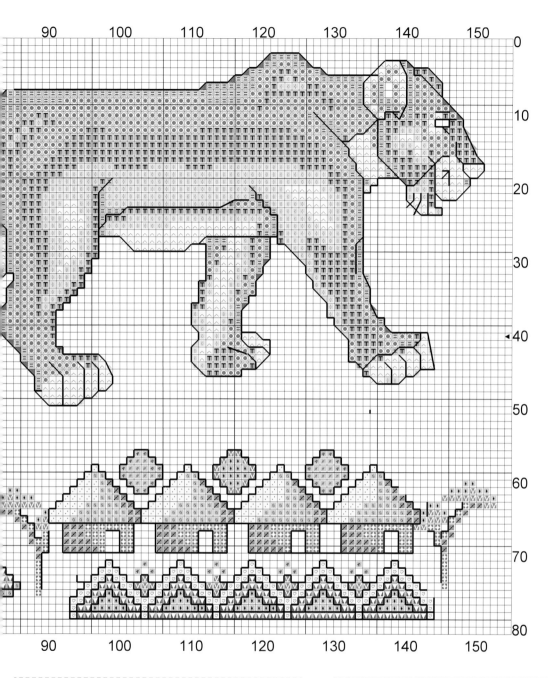

		Anchor	Madeira
⋀	Cream	826	2101
T	Tan med lt	362	2012
◊	Tan vy lt	1009	2014
◆	Pistachio Green vy lt	1043	1309
◉	Tan med	1045	2011
⊟	Brown vy lt	1046	2010
V	Pistachio Green lt	214	1310
☐	Black	403	Black

		Anchor	Madeira
▽	Green med	210	1407
·•·	Off White	386	0101
♡	White	1	White
G	Autumn Gold lt	301	2309
✦	Autumn Gold dk	1003	0310
⊘	Yellow lt	301	0110
◿	Autumn Gold	323	2514
⅂	Yellow med	305	0113

Lion's Den

A lion pride, made up of about two males and four females, occupies a territory which is protected by the males so that the lionesses can breed freely. Quite often a young male lion will be forced out of a pride when conditions are bad, and becomes nomadic. When a vacancy exists in a territory through the death or disappearance of a pride male these nomadic male lions can lay claim to a territory. The lion's roar tells other male lions when a vacancy exists so that he can approach and fight for acceptance.

Lion's Den special notes

If you need any reminders, refer to General Instructions for Working a Design on page 28.

This design has been stitched on 28 count linen fabric using 3 strands of thread in a size 24 needle for cross stitch and 1 strand in a size 26 needle for backstitch. The 28 count linen is the equivalent of 14 count Aida.

If you are using linen it is advisable to wash it in hot water before you begin the embroidery to pre-shrink it. Follow instructions for stitching on linen or evenweave.

You will need

• Stranded cotton as per key

• Tapestry needles
size 24 (cross stitch)
size 26 (backstitch)

• Linen fabric 28 count
26 cm (10.2 in) square

Design size

• 75 x 74 stitches
Aida 11 count = 17.3 x 17.1 cm (6.8 x 6.7 in)
Aida 14 count = 13.6 x 13.4 cm (5.4 x 5.3 in)
Aida 18 count = 10.6 x 10.4 cm (4.2 x 4.1 in)

		DMC
✖	Cornflower Blue lt	794
⬢	Cornflower Blue med	793
◖	Cornflower Blue dk	792
✚	Chartreuse bright	704
Ⓝ	Chartreuse	703
◪	Christmas Green lt	702
2	Topaz vy lt	727
—	Topaz lt	726
◣	Topaz	725
Ɛ	Golden Brown vy lt	3827
=	Golden Brown lt	977
◉	Golden Brown med	976
◎	Golden Brown med dk	3826
♡	White	Blanc
☐	Black	310

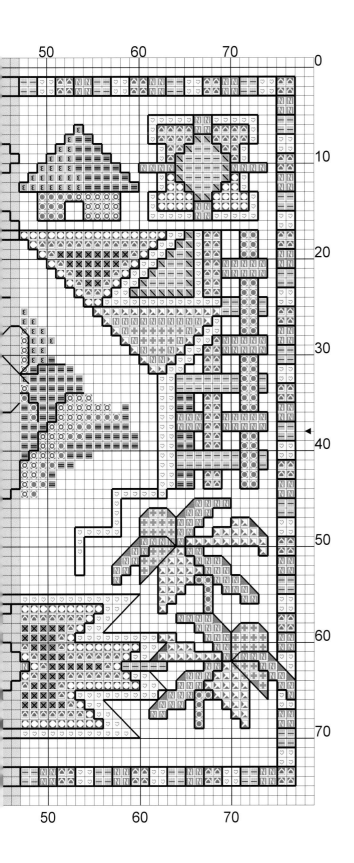

		Anchor	Madeira
✗	Cornflower Blue lt	175	0907
⬠	Cornflower Blue med	176	0906
◖	Cornflower Blue dk	177	0905
✚	Chartreuse bright	256	1308
N	Chartreuse	238	1307
◨	Christmas Green lt	226	1306
2	Topaz vy lt	293	0110
▬	Topaz lt	297	0109
◥	Topaz	305	0106
ε	Golden Brown vy lt	363	2301
▬	Golden Brown lt	1002	2307
◉	Golden Brown med	308	2302
◎	Golden Brown med dk	1049	2306
♡	White	1	White
☐	Black	403	Black

Guineafowl on Parade

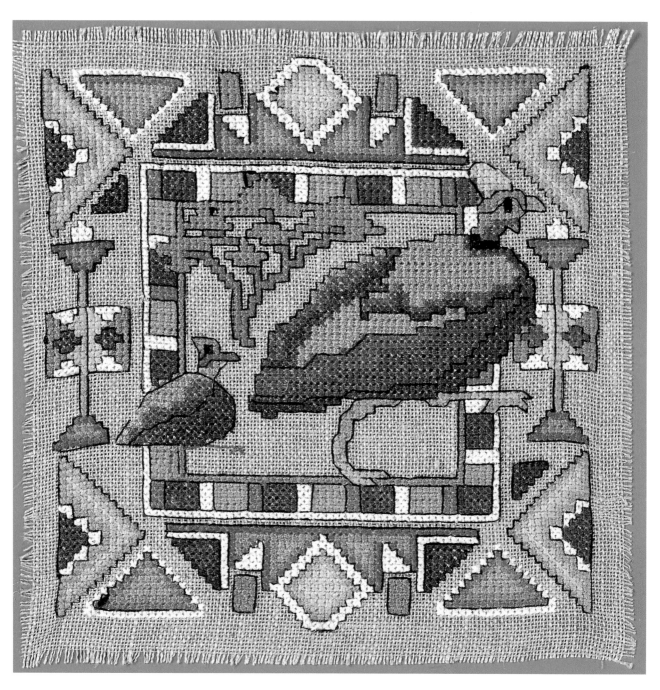

The helmeted guineafowl are usually found in flocks except during the breeding season, when they are seen in family groups led by parents with the children in tow. They feed on seeds and insects and spend most of the time on the ground but can fly when necessary. This design can be used to stitch a picture, cushion, sling bag or any suitable item of your choice.

Guineafowl on Parade special notes

If you need any reminders, refer to General Instructions for Working a Design on page 28.

This design has been stitched on 28 count linen fabric using 3 strands of thread in a size 24 needle for cross stitch and 1 strand in a size 26 needle for backstitch. The 28 count linen is the equivalent of 14 count Aida. French knots on the guineafowl are worked in white using 2 strands of thread.

If using linen it is advisable to wash it in hot water first to pre-shrink it. Follow instructions for stitching on linen or evenweave.

The French knots are worked at random on the guineafowl only; refer to the photograph for placement.

Wash completed work in cool water and iron face down on a fluffy towel.

Mount the picture or make up the item of your choice as directed in the finishing instructions section.

You will need

• Stranded cotton as per key
• Tapestry needles
size 24 (cross stitch)
size 26 (backstitch)
• Linen fabric 28 count
26 cm (10.2 in) square

Design size

• 79 x 80 stitches
Aida 11 count =
18.2 x 18.5 cm (7.2 x 7.3 in)
Aida 14 count = 1
4.3 x 14.5 cm (5.6 x 5.7 in)
Aida 18 count =
11.1 x 11.3 cm (4.4 x 4.4 in)

		DMC
⊟	Baby Blue med	334
⊖	Navy Blue vy lt	322
▽	Navy lt	312
◐	Navy Blue med dk	336
N	Gold	783
—	Topaz lt	726
◥	Topaz	725
✦	Copper vy lt	922
◨	Copper lt	921
⊓	Copper med	920
◖	Red Copper	919
!	White bright	B5200
◩	Christmas Green lt	702
☐	Black	310

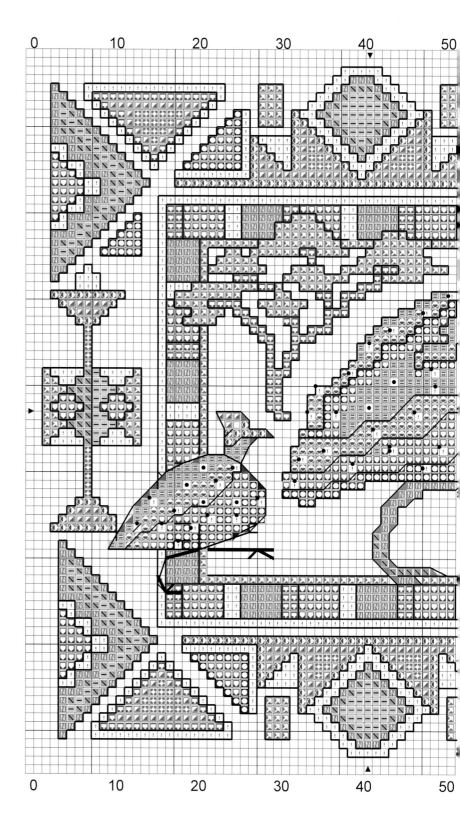

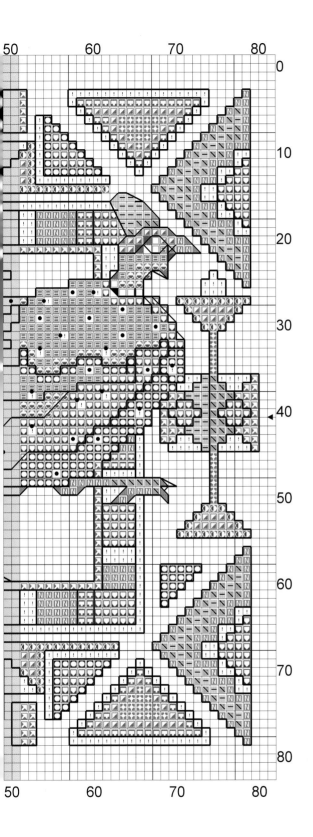

		Anchor	Madeira
⊟	Baby Blue med	977	1003
⬤	Navy Blue vy lt	978	1004
▽	Navy lt	147	1005
◖	Navy Blue med dk	149	1007
N	Gold	307	2211
–	Topaz lt	297	0109
◨	Topaz	305	0106
✦	Copper vy lt	1003	0311
◿	Copper lt	1003	0311
⊓	Copper med	1004	0312
◑	Red Copper	340	0313
!	White bright	1	White
◪	Christmas Green lt	226	1306
☐	Black	403	Black

Giraffe at Waterhole

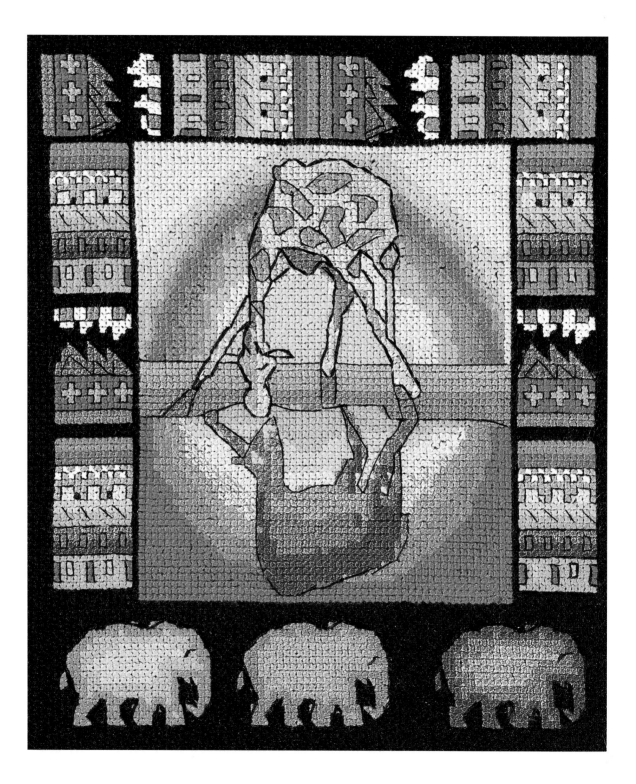

A waterhole or pan is formed by elephants when their massive bodies sink down into wet soil causing soggy depressions which eventually form deep pools of water. A whole community of wildlife meets daily at these waterholes to drink, play or just wallow. This design can be used to stitch a picture, bag cover, cushion cover or any other item of your choice.

Giraffe at Waterhole special notes

If you need any reminders, refer to General Instructions for Working a Design on page 28.

This design has been stitched on 14 count Aida fabric using 3 strands of thread in a size 24 needle for cross stitch. Use 2 strands of black in a size 26 needle to outline the giraffe itself in backstitch, but only 1 strand to outline the reflection and other elements.

If using linen it is advisable to wash it before use in hot water to pre-shrink it. Follow instructions for stitching on linen or evenweave.

Wash completed work in cool water and iron face down on a fluffy towel.

Mount as a picture or make up into another item as directed in the finishing instructions section.

You will need

• Stranded cotton as per key
• Tapestry needles
size 24 (cross stitch)
size 26 (backstitch)
• Aida fabric 14 count
26 x 30 cm (10 x 12 in)

Design size

• 84 x 101 stitches
11 count = 19.4 x 23.3 cm
(7.6 x 9.2 in)
14 count = 15.2 x 18.3 cm
(7 x 7.2 in)
18 count = 11.9 x 14.3 cm
(4.7 x 5.6 in)

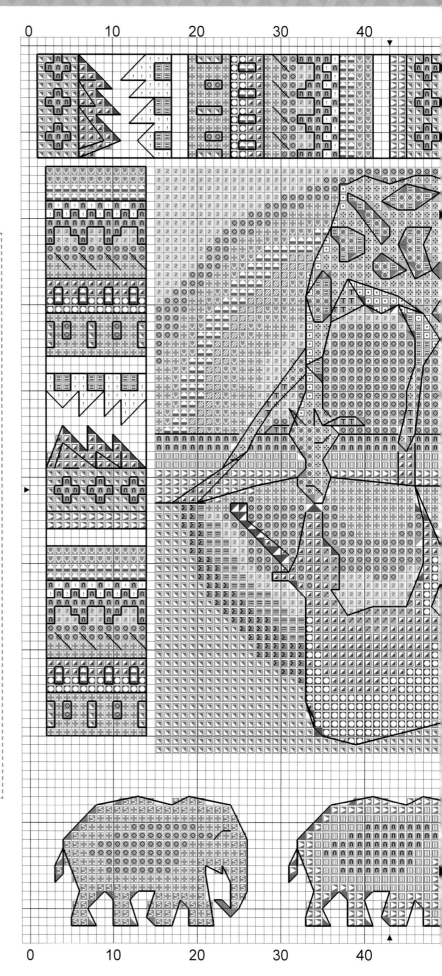

		DMC
❖	Tan lt	738
T	Tan med lt	437
⊙	Tan med	436
▤	Brown vy lt	435
▫	Brown lt	434
▨	Orange Red med dk	946
∩	Chartreuse bright	704
⫴	Chartreuse	703
▷	Christmas Green lt	702
!	White bright	B5200
Σ	Bright Turquoise lt	6846
═	Blue + Turquoise lt	3811 + 3846
◥	Bright Turquoise	3844
◠	Christmas Red lt	3801
2	Topaz vy lt	727
◇	Topaz	725
✛	Tangerine med	741
∨	Orange Red med	947
S	Orange	740
↗	Delft	809
◢	Delft dk	798
○	Royal Blue med	797

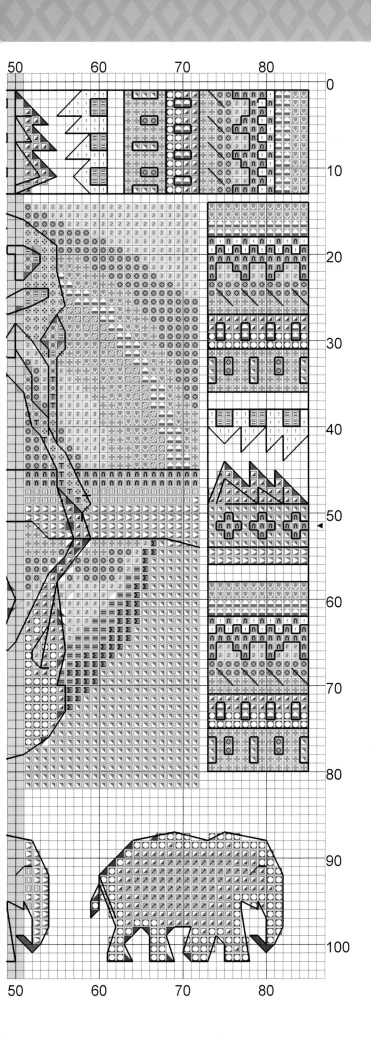

		Anchor	Madeira
⬩⠶	Tan lt	942	2013
T	Tan med lt	362	2012
◐	Tan med	1045	2011
▣	Brown vy lt	1046	2010
▪	Brown lt	310	2009
▨	Orange Red med dk	332	0206
⋒	Chartreuse bright	256	1308
▥	Chartreuse	238	1307
▶	Christmas Green lt	226	1306
!	White bright	1	White
Σ	Bright Turquoise lt	1089	1103
=	Blue + Turquoise lt	928	1104
◣	Bright Turquoise	410	1110
⌒	Christmas Red lt	46	0411
2	Topaz vy lt	293	0110
◇	Topaz	305	0106
✛	Tangerine med	314	0201
⋁	Orange Red med	330	0205
⑤	Orange		
↗	Delft	130	0909
◢	Delft dk	137	0911
◖	Royal Blue med	147	091

Sunshine Sampler

This sampler can be stitched into a picture, cushion or any suitable item.

You might wish to replace the patterns within the central panel with the wording of your choice, using the alphabet chart following.

Sunshine Sampler special notes

If you need any reminders, refer to General Instructions for Working a Design on page 28.

This design has been stitched on 28 count linen fabric using 3 strands of thread in a size 24 needle for cross stitch and 1 strand of black in a size 26 needle for backstitch.

If using linen it is advisable to wash it in hot water first to pre-shrink it. See instructions for stitching linen.

Work French knots randomly over guinea fowl body in white—see photo for placement.

Wash finished embroidery in cool water and iron face down on a fluffy towel.

Complete the picture or item of your choice as directed in the finishing instructions section.

You will need

• Stranded cotton as per key

• Tapestry needles

size 24 (cross stitch)

size 26 (backstitch)

• Linen fabric 28 count

32 cm (13 in) square

Design size

• 121 x 131 stitches

Aida 11 count = 27.9 x 30.2 cm

(11 x 11.9 in)

Aida 14 count = 22 x 23.8 cm

(8.6 x 9.4 in)

Aida 18 count = 17.1 x 18.5 cm

(6.7 x 7.3 in)

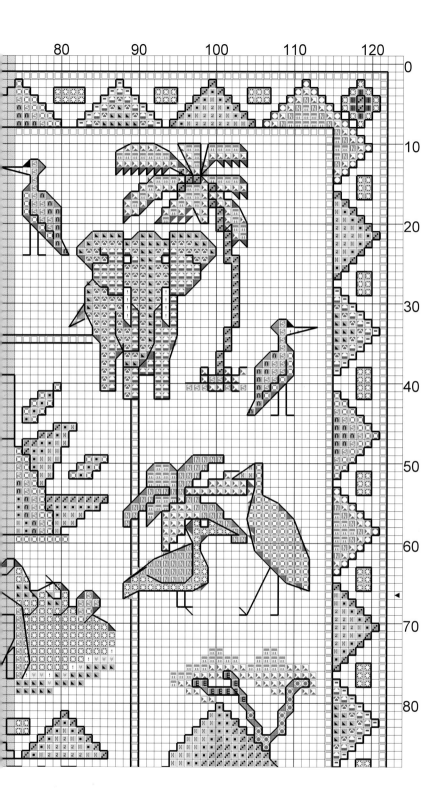

		DMC
⊠	Christmas red lt	891
Ⅲ	Blue Violet	340
✳	Blue Violet med	3746
◣	Blue Violet lt	341
⬠	Cornflower Blue med	793
⬡	Cornflower Blue dk	792
⊟	Cornflower Blue vy dk	791
⊞	Charteuse bright	704
Ɲ	Chartreuse	703
⊠	Christmas Green lt	702
◯	Christmas Green med	701
■	Gold	783
2	Topaz vy lt	727
⋈	Topaz lt	726
■	Topaz	725
∩	Orange Spice lt	722
Ƨ	Orange Spice med	721
Ɛ	Golden Brown vy lt	3827
=	Golden Brown lt	977
⊞	Golden brown med	976
◎	Golden Brown med dk	3826
E	Beige brown med	840
⁘	Beige Brown dk	839
◉	Beige Brown vy dk	938
!	White bright	B5200
≽	Pearl grey	415
◥	Steel Grey dk	414
☐	Black	310

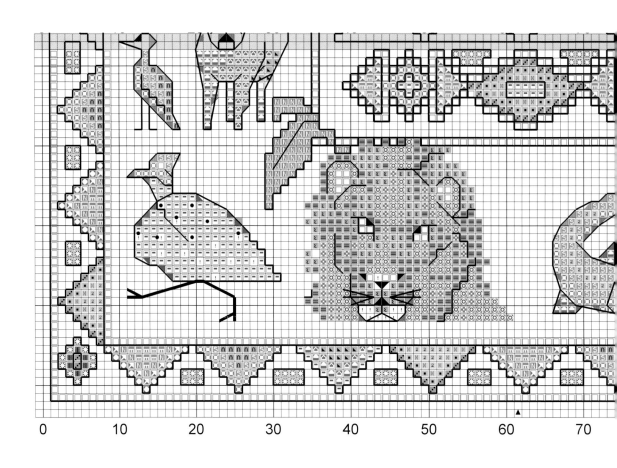

0   10   20   30   40   50   60   70

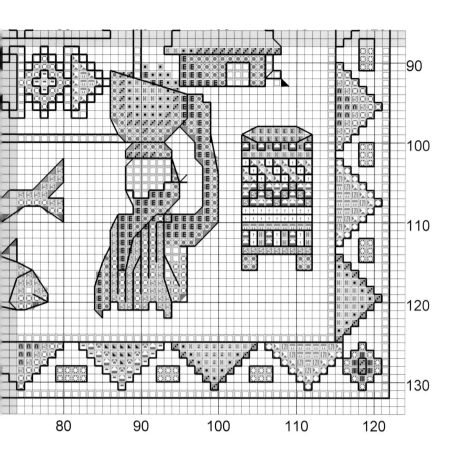

		Anchor	Madeira
	Christmas red lt	29	0411
	Blue Violet	118	0902
	Blue Violet med	1030	0903
	Blue Violet lt	117	0901
	Cornflower Blue med	176	0906
	Cornflower Blue dk	177	0905
	Cornflower Blue vy dk	123	0904
	Charteuse bright	256	1308
N	Chartreuse	238	1307
	Christmas Green lt	226	1306
	Christmas Green med	227	1305
	Gold	307	2211
2	Topaz vy lt	293	0110
H	Topaz lt	297	0109

		Anchor	Madeira
■	Topaz	305	0106
n	Orange Spice lt	323	0307
S	Orange Spice med	324	0308
E	Golden Brown vy lt	363	2301
=	Golden Brown lt	1002	2307
	Golden brown med	308	2302
◎	Golden Brown med dk	1049	23096
E	Beige brown med	379	1912
	Beige Brown dk	1050	1913
◉	Beige Brown vy dk	381	2003
!	White bright	1	White
⩔	Pearl grey	398	1802
◣	Steel Grey dk	235	1801
☐	Black	403	Black

Motifs

Here are 25 motifs which you can use to make up your own designs.

		DMC	Anchor	Madeira
	Topaz vy lt	727	293	0110
	Golden brown med	976	308	2302
	White bright	B5200	1	White
	Black	310	403	Black
	Golden brown vy lt	3827	363	2301
	Golden brown med dk	3826	1049	2306
	Golden Brown med	976	308	2302
	Yellow med	743	305	0113
	Golden Brown lt	977	1002	2307
	Tangerine lt	742	303	0107
	Winter White	3865	2	White
	Tangerine dk	740	316	0202
	Tangerine med	741	314	0201
	Steel Grey dk	414	235	1801
	Chartreuse bright	704	256	1308
	Golden Brown vy lt	3827	363	2301
	Golden Brown lt	977	1002	2307
	Golden Brown med dk	3826	1049	2306

		DMC	Anchor	Madeira
	Beige Brown	841	378	1911
	Topaz lt	726	297	0109
	Old Gold vy lt	677	886	2207
	Old Gold dk	680	907	2210
	Baby Blue med	334	977	1003
	Old Gold lt	676	891	2208
	Old Gold med	729	890	2012
	Blue Violet lt	341	117	0901
	Cornflower Blue med	793	176	0906
	Cornflower Blue dk	792	177	0905
	Christmas Red lt	891	29	0411
	Orange Spice lt	722	323	0307
	Orange Spice med	721	324	0308
	Christmas Green lt	702	226	1306
	Steel grey dk	414	235	1801
	Topaz lt	726	297	0109
	Beige Brown vy dk	938	381	2003

Motifs

		DMC	Anchor	Madeira
	Golden Brown med	976	308	2302
	White bright	B5200	1	White
	Black	310	403	Black
	Christmas Red lt	891	29	0411
	Orange Spice med	721	324	0308
	Christmas Green lt	702	226	1306
	Topaz lt	726	297	0109
	Beige Brown vy dk	938	381	2003
	Gold	783	307	2211
	Topaz	725	305	0106
	Beige brown med	840	379	1912
	Cornflower Blue med	793	176	0906

		DMC	Anchor	Madeira
	Blue Violet lt	341	117	0901
	Cornflower Blue dk	792	177	0905
	Cornflower Blue vy dk	791	123	0904
	Blue Violet Med	3746	1030	0903
	Pearl Grey	415	398	1802
	Chartreuse bright	704	256	1308
	Golden Brown vy lt	3827	363	2301
	Golden Brown lt	977	1002	2307
	Golden Brown med dk	3826	1049	2306
	Steel Grey dk	414	235	1801
	Beige Brown dk	839	1050	1913
	Orange Spice	722	323	0307

Motifs

		DMC	Anchor	Madeira
	Topaz lt	726	297	0109
	Golden Brown med	976	308	2302
	Tan lt	738	942	2013
	White	Blanc	1	White
	Black	310	403	Black
	Blue Violet lt	341	117	0901
	Cornflower Blue med	793	176	0906
	Cornflower Blue dk	792	177	0905
	Orange Spice med	721	324	0308
	Christmas Green lt	702	226	1306
	Chartreuse	703	238	1307
	Pearl Grey	415	398	1802
	Tangerine lt	742	303	0107
	Tangerine dk	740	316	0202
	Yellow ultra vy lt	3823	386	0111

		DMC	Anchor	Madeira
	Yellow by lt	745	300	0111
	Yellow lt	744	301	0110
	Tan med lt	437	362	2012
	Tan med	436	1045	2011
	Golden Brown vy lt	3827	363	2301
	Golden Brown lt	977	1002	2307
	Golden Brown med dk	3826	1049	2306
	Christmas Green med	701	227	1305
	Gold	783	307	2211
	Golden Brown med dk	3826	1049	2306
	Topaz	725	305	0106
	Tangerine med	741	314	0201
	Orange Red med	947	330	0205
	Chartreuse bright	704	256	1308
	Navy Blue med dk	336	149	1007

Alphabet Chart

For use with samplers and cards.

A B C D E F G H I J K L M
N O P Q R S T U V W X Y Z
1 2 3 4 5 6 7 8 9 0

A B C D E F G H I J K L M
N O P Q R S T U V W X Y Z
1 2 3 4 5 6 7 8 9 0

ON YOUR WEDDING

WELCOME

WELL DONE

CONGRATS

GOOD LUCK

HAPPY BIRTHDAY

ON YOUR SPECIAL DAY

ENGAGEMENT ANNIVERSARY

YOU PASSED

THANKYOU

BEST WISHES

JUST FOR YOU

THINKING OF YOU

HELLO

Acknowledgements

As always, many people must be acknowledged for their help in producing a book—whether emotional support, encouragement, or hands-on help, they are all contributing factors.

Ricky and Pat deserve special mention, as they have been a part of *The African Cross Stitch Collection* since the beginning. Ricky, we never did get to Mauritius but the journey we shared and the friendship we forged were just as memorable—thanks for everything. Pat, I could not have done any of this without you, thanks for all the effort and support on behalf of *The African Cross Stitch Collection* overseas, for help with the suppliers index and for numerous supplies sent; this is our book.

The African Cross Stitch Collection is dedicated to the memory of Maureen, who passed on just before it was published—it could not have succeeded without your enthusiasm and positive attitude. We all miss you.

My thanks to Sue for illustrations, and to Nigel for help with computer graphics and your immense support. Thanks to Joneta for all your help in Cape Town.

My thanks go to Dollfus Mieg et Cie (DMC) in France for the assistance, support and encouragement proffered before and during the writing of this book. Thank you for allowing us the mention of your worldwide distributors and for the use of DMC products throughout this book.

As always, many thanks to Libby Renney, Sally Milner Publishing, for making this book possible and for putting it together so beautifully, and to Riana Van Der Merwe of Threads & Crafts magazine for putting us on the map in South Africa and for all her support and advice.

Special thanks go to the people in my life who offer support and encouragement in their individual ways—my family. Mum and Dad, you are always there for me, we will have many more happy times together in this new chapter of our lives. (Dad, don't forget the tool box!) Mum Burr and Sue, always so encouraging, we will always be next door in mind. Boo, John, Devon and Georgia in New Zealand, and Gordon, Wendy, Ash, Ben and Nix who are now in Australia, we will always be a united family and no distance can change that. To my husband Simon who never stops believing in me, pays all the bills and makes all things possible, this book marks the start of a new journey together; and to my special girls, Stacey, Tessa and Katie, who are the centre of my world, thank you for being you.

I will publish the name of the Lord: ascribe ye greatness unto our God (Deut 32:1).

Suppliers Index

There are numerous stitching shops, Internet sites and mail order companies that will supply embroidery threads, needles, stitching fabrics and accessories. The DMC distributors listed here will be happy to provide you with the name of a stockist in your area. Alternatively, you can log on to www.dmc.com; this site has a store search facility that will give you all the stores in your area throughout the world.

Asia
DMC Creative World Pte. Ltd
60 Martin Road
#02-06 TradeMart Singapore
Singapore 239065
Tel: 65-732-9931

Australia
Radda Pty Ltd
51-55 Carrington Road
Marrickville NSW 2204
Tel: +61 2 9559 3088

Brazil
DMC Creative World Do Brasil Ltda
Rua 1101, No 60
Camboriu Business Center
Sala 164
B. Camboriu SC
Tel: 55-47-366 6077

Benelux – Germany/Scandinavia
DMC S.A.
Avenue des pagodes 1–3
1–3 Pagodenlaan
1020 Bruxelles/Brussels
Tel: 32.2.240.10.30

France
DMC
Service Consommateur
13 Rue de Pfastatt
68057 Mulhouse Cedex
Tel: 03 89 32 45 28

Italy
DMC
Viale Italia 84
20020 Lainate MI
Tel: 39-02-935 704 27

Japan
Dmc k.k.
Akazawa Building 6F
2-10-10, Kotobuki, Taito Ku
Tokyo 111
Tel: 8-3-5828 4112

Portugal
DMC
Travessa da Escola Araujo 36-A
1150 Lisbonne
Tel: 351-21-317 28 80

South Africa
DMC Creative World (Pty) Ltd
Hill's Building
Buchanan Square
162 Sir Lowry Road
8001 Cape Town
Tel: 27-21-461 9482

Spain
DMC
Fontanella. 21-23 5o 4a
08010 Barcelona
Tel: 34-93-317 74 36

United Kingdom
DMC Creative World Ltd
Pullman Road, Wigston
Leicestershire LEI8 2DY
Tel: 44 116-2 81 10 40

United States
The DMC Corporation
10 Port Kearny
South Kearny NJ 07032
Tel: 1-973-589 0606